CLIMBING AND HIKING IN ECUADOR

Antisana.

Climbing and Hiking in Ecuador

Rob Rachowiecki

BRADT PUBLICATIONS, UK
HUNTER PUBLISHING, USA

DEDICATION
To my parents, Alec and Rene Rachowiecki, with love and gratitude

First published in 1984 by Bradt Publications, 41 Nortoft Road, Chalfont St Peter, Bucks SL9 0LA, England.
   Distributed in the USA by Hunter Publishing Inc., 300 Raritan Center Parkway, CN94, Edison, NJ 08818.

British Library Cataloguing in Publication Data

Rachowiecki, Rob
   Climbing and hiking in Ecuador.
   1. Rock climbing—Ecuador
   I. Title
   796.5'22   GV199.44.E/

ISBN 0-9505797-2-6

Library of Congress Cataloging in Publication data
Rachowiecki, Rob, 1954–
   Climbing and hiking in Ecuador.

   Bibliography: p.
   Includes index.
   1. Mountaineering – Ecuador – Guide-books.   2. Hiking – Ecuador – Guide-books.   3. Ecuador – Description and travel – 1981–   – Guide-books.   I. Title.
   GV199.44.E2R33   1982   918.66'0474   83-25712
   ISBN 0-933982-23-2 (U.S.)

Engravings from *Travels Amongst the Great Andes of the Equator* by Edward Whymper, originally published in 1891 by John Murray.
Poems from *Ecuador, a Travel Journal* by Henri Michaux, published by Peter Owen, 1970. Reproduced by kind permission of the publishers.
Maps by Hans Van Well.
Cover photo by the author: View from Cotopaxi.

Printed in Great Britain by A. Wheaton & Co. Ltd., Exeter

ACKNOWLEDGEMENTS

Many people in Ecuador helped me in researching and writing this book. I am particularly grateful to Mike Hooper, who not only gave me his house to stay in, but also managed to nearly demolish two 4WD vehicles in his attempts to get me up the mountains and, when all else failed, accompanied me to the top of several on foot.

Other hikers and climbers who accompanied me on my many mountaineering fiascos and occasional successes were Susan Alexander and Paul Dutch (Chimborazo area hikes and Carihuairazo ascents); Geoff Bartram of the American Alpine Institute with Chris Curry (Cotacachi, Las Cajas and the Inca Trail to Ingapirca); Ivan Castaigne (Iliniza Norte, Cayambe and useful verbal information); Myles Conway and Dave (Reventador and various foolish ventures into the jungle); Jim Desrossiers and Roberto Fuentes (El Altar); Alan Klingenstein (Andes to Jungle Hike and verbal abuse); Steve McFarland, ex-president of the now defunct International Andean Mountaineering Club (various excursions); Michael Orr (Cotopaxi, Cayambe, Imbabura, El Altar, Iliniza Sur); Carol from the US who walked around Cotopaxi; Big Al who climbed Tungurahua and ate 20 boiled eggs in a weekend; and various other people whose names I've misplaced but who helped in many adventures.

It's more than just support in the mountains that helps get a book written. Many people helped me in Quito and elsewhere with hospitality and information. Thank you to Pieter von Bunningen, Alan Cathey, Carol Dennison, Dr Minard "Pete" Hall, Elaine Hooper, Helena Landázuri of the Fundación Natura, Alan Miller, and various Peace Corps volunteers, especially Tom in Mulaló and the gang in Tena.

Licenciado Gabriel Pazmiño and Isabel Oviedo both helped tremendously with obtaining my visa extensions in Quito – without their help this book would never have been started.

Michael Kelsey and Michael Koerner, whose books are listed in the bibliography, reviewed and criticized my manuscript in its early stages, and Pieter Crow and Kevin Healey wrote useful letters about various aspects of Ecuadorian mountaineering.

Mike Shawcross read the proofs, and Dr Cathy Payson checked the health section.

My parents provided me with work space and a typewriter during the two all too short months I spent in England transcribing my field notes into the finished product.

For some reason, the person who deserves the greatest thanks and praise always gets left until the end. Adequate acknowledgement cannot be given to Hilary Bradt, editor, publisher, and good friend, who never flagged in supporting me in this venture.

Sincere thanks to you all.

THE HIGHLANDS
OF ECUADOR

CONTENTS

INTRODUCTION . . . . . WHY ECUADOR?

Though one of the smallest countries in South America, Ecuador offers an incredible diversity of scenery, wildlife and people. The mountaineer and adventurous traveller have a choice of the ice-clad Andes, tropical rainforest, mountain trails leading to Inca ruins, and quiet beaches; and all these attractions lie within a day's journey of Quito, the capital city. This accessibility makes Ecuador an attractive destination for climbers and hikers of all abilities, and avoids the long approaches and expedition planning often necessary in other high mountain ranges.

Mountaineers find Ecuador well suited as a high altitude training ground. There are many technically straightforward ascents of 5000-metre peaks. Climbers can gain technical experience in the lower ranges of Europe and North America and then learn about how the body functions at high altitudes in the Ecuadorian Andes. A combination of these abilities will produce climbers ready to challenge some of the world's most difficult high peaks.

Superb mountain scenery is only one of Ecuador's attractions. It has some of the best beaches in South America, colourful Indian markets, and plenty of wildlife, especially birds. Come and see for yourself.

Carihuairazo from the south.

CHAPTER 1
ECUADOR:
GENERAL INFORMATION

GEOGRAPHY

Geographically, Ecuador is one of the most varied countries in the world, despite its small size (283,520 sq km, only a little larger than Great Britain).

The Andean range is at its narrowest here and divides the country into three distinct regions. To the east of the Central Sierra lies the tropical rainforest of the upper Amazon basin (known as the Oriente) and to the west are the more accessible but equally hot and humid coastal lowlands. It is barely 200 km from the western lowlands to the eastern jungle, yet within this narrow area are found peaks to 6310 m forming two major *cordilleras* or mountain ranges.

The two cordilleras run north–south and are 40 to 60 km apart. Between them lies the fertile Central Valley which is about 400 km long and contains Quito and most of Ecuador's major cities as well as almost half of the country's inhabitants. It is this Central Valley that was called "The Avenue of the Volcanoes" by the famous German explorer and scientist, Alexander von Humboldt, who visited Ecuador in 1802.

GEOLOGY

Ecuador has one of the world's greatest concentrations of volcanoes. There are over thirty, of which at least eight are considered to be active.

The Eastern Cordillera, sometimes known as the Cordillera Real, is older and (on average) higher and larger than the Western Cordillera. Base rock is mainly gneiss, mica-schist and other crystalline rocks, but constant and heavy volcanic activity has covered the area with plenty of volcanic material and resulted in several classically cone shaped volcanoes of which Cotopaxi (5897 m) is particularly famous. Several smaller peaks, not of volcanic origin, are found on the eastern slopes of this *cordillera* pushing their way out of the jungles of the Oriente, and further to the east other isolated mountains are completely separated from the Eastern Cordillera by jungle. The most important are Reventador (3485 m) and Sumaco (3900 m) both of which are active and relatively inaccessible volcanoes.

Although Ecuador's highest peak, the dormant volcano Chimborazo (6310 m) is part of the Western Cordillera, this range is not generally as massive as the Eastern. It is made of porphyritic eruptive rocks of the Mesozoic age, and intense volcanic activity has covered it with volcanic material to an even greater extent than the Eastern Cordillera.

HISTORY

Very little is known of the earliest history of the area. In the early 1400s at least six linguistic groups were recognized in the highlands alone (the Pasto, Cara, Panzaleo, Puruhá, Cañari, and Palta) and by the middle of the century the Caras had gained a dominant position. They overpowered a minor tribe, the Quitus (hence Quito), forming the kingdom of the Shyris which was the major presence in the area at the time of Inca expansion from the south. Despite several years of resistance, the Shyris and nearby lesser groups were integrated into the Inca empire by about 1490.

In 1525 the Inca Huayna Capac died, dividing his empire between two sons. Atahualpa, of Shyri descent on his mother's side, became ruler of the northern part of the empire, whilst Huáscar received the rest. Violent civil war between the two brothers followed which Atahualpa won. Thus when the Spanish conquest began in 1532 the Inca Empire had been severely weakened by the civil war. Atahualpa was captured and paid a huge ransom in gold and silver for his release; despite this he was murdered by Pizarro and the Inca Empire effectively came to an end.

In 1534 Sebastián de Benalcázar founded Quito on the ruins of the old Shyri city. After the success of the Spanish conquest the area became known as the Audiencia de Quito, and (except for a period of 6 years) remained under the viceroy of Peru until 1740 when it became part of the Viceroyalty of Nueva Granada. The sixteenth to eighteenth centuries were characterized by peaceful colonialism. Agriculture was developed, the Indians were exploited, and Spain profited.

By the nineteenth century a strong independence movement had developed in common with other parts of South America. From 1809 several unsuccessful attempts at independence were made but it was not until May 24 1822 that Mariscal Sucre finally defeated the royalist forces at the Battle of Pichincha. Although free of the Spanish, the area now became part of Gran Colombia and it took over 8 more years before Ecuador became completely independent under the leadership of the first president, General Juan José Flores.

The rest of the nineteenth century was a continuous struggle between conservatives and liberals. By the end of the 1800s Ecuador was under the military rule of General Eloy Alfaro and much of the twentieth century has been a succession of unstable military governments. A civilian leader, President Jaime Roldós, was elected in 1979 and after his untimely death in an air accident was succeeded by Vice-President Osvaldo Hurtado Larrea who is in office at the time of writing.

PEOPLE
A census held in 1982 revealed that Ecuador's population had reached 8,945,000. This is approximately eleven times the number of Indians estimated to have been living in the area at the time of the Spanish conquest. The population density of almost 32 people per sq km is the highest in South America.

About 40% of this total are Indians and an equal number are *mestizos* (mixed Spanish/Indian stock). About 10% are white and the remainder black or Asian.

The majority of the Indians are Quechua speaking and live in the highlands; they are the direct descendants of the inhabitants of the Inca Empire. There are also several small groups living in the lowlands and speaking their own distinct languages. These tribes include, among others, the Shuar (Jivaro), Auca, Cofan, and Secoya of the Oriente and the Cayapa and the Colorado Indians of the coastal plain. The highland Indians are often bilingual, although Spanish is a second language and not much used in remote areas. Until land reforms of the 1960s the majority of the Quechua Indians were little more than slaves to the big *hacienda* owners. Nowadays they are developing co-operatives and own land but nevertheless live at a subsistence level in many cases.

Some groups, notably the Otavalo Indians and to a lesser extent the Salasacas and Cañars, have made a successful reputation as excellent weavers and craftsmen and their goods are in great demand. After some time in Ecuador you will notice the different styles of clothing that individual groups traditionally wear. The Otavalo men are characterized by their white, calf-length trousers, rope sandals, grey or blue ponchos, and long single braid of hair. The women wear a colourfully embroidered blouse and a bulky gold-coloured necklace. The Salasaca men wear distinctive broad brimmed white hats, white shirts, and black ponchos. The Indians of the Saquisilí area are most often seen wearing red ponchos and little felt 'pork pie' hats.

Another interesting and attractive feature of Indian life is the fiestas which often celebrate church holidays. One of my favourite fiestas is that of All Souls Day (November 2) when throngs of people visit cemeteries to pay their respects to the dead. Everyone does this, from rich *Quiteños* to poor *campesinos* (peasants), but the cemeteries near the Indian villages are the most colourful. Hundreds of people show up in their best clothes and leave wreaths and flowers on the graves. To ensure that their departed friends and relatives also enjoy the day the people bring food and drink and leave some in remembrance and offering. The majority of the food and drink is, of course, consumed by the Indians themselves and the atmosphere is generally festive rather than sombre.

CLIMATE

Most descriptions of Ecuador's climate agree that its most reliable aspect is its unreliability. Unfortunately, this really seems to be the case, so I can't give you foolproof advice on which months will be best for your visit. However, here are some generalizations.

In common with other tropical countries, Ecuador does not experience the four seasons known in temperate parts of the world. Instead there are wet and dry seasons. Despite its small size, Ecuador has several distinct climatic zones with wet and dry periods varying from area to area.

The coastal areas are influenced by the cold Humboldt current which flows up from the south Pacific, but during December a warm current from the north, seasonably called 'El Niño' (the Christ Child) predominates. This marks the beginning of the coastal rainy season. The northern coast is wet from January to June and dryish for the rest of the year, while further south the coast experiences a shorter wet season and in the dry season, from May to December, it is much drier than in the north. The effects of 'El Niño' are not yet fully understood, and in some years there are devastating floods in the coastal lowlands during the wet season.

Inland, the climate is completely different. It rains most of the time in the Oriente though some months are a little less wet than others, depending on the area. The weather in the mountains varies from east to west. The eastern mountains, especially Antisana, El Altar and Sangay, and to a lesser extent Cayambe and Tungurahua are influenced by air from the Amazonian lowlands. The wettest months are June through August. December and January are when the highest number of successful ascents have been made on the difficult El Altar. Ecuadorian climbers favour February for climbing Antisana and October through January are suggested for Cayambe.

The situation is reversed in the western mountains. Here, the dry season is late June through early September, with a short dry spell in December and early January. The wettest months are February to May with April being the wettest of all. Edward Whymper claims to have spent 78 days in the vicinity of Iliniza during February to April of 1880 ". . . yet we did not see the whole of the mountain on any single occasion." During the dry season temperatures tend to be very low at night and high winds can be a problem, particularly in August.

The weather in October and November tends to be variable. Snow build-up during these months sometimes provides quite good snow conditions for the short December–January season.

The temperature variation is mainly influenced by altitude. From sea level to about 900 m it is hot with an average temperature of 26°–28°C. The warm zone is from 900 m to 2000 m with an average temperature range of 20°–26°C. From 2000 m to 3000 m it is quite cold with an average of 12°–20°C. (Remember average includes warm afternoons and freezing nights.) Above 3000 m is the *páramo* with temperatures averaging from 0°–12°C and above the lowest snow line at about 4500 m the mean temperature stays below freezing, although the strong sun sometimes makes it feel much warmer.

There have been noticeable recent changes in the world's climatic patterns and Ecuador has been experiencing a period of relative drought compared with a century ago (although this is difficult to believe when you are caught in a torrential Ecuadorian downpour). This has also contributed to the receding glaciers on Ecuador's mountains. Some people also claim that sun-spot and other solar activity affects the climate in a seven to eleven year cycle. Certainly, a year of greater precipitation is experienced at irregular intervals. Although proper detailed records have been kept only since about the 1960s, it is known that the periods 1965, 1972/3 and 1975/6, and 1982/3 have been particularly wet. This cycle is said to be wet to begin with and drier in later years; the drier years mean a significant reduction or disappearance of glaciers. 1981 was the last year of the most recent cycle and many mountains which have permanent glaciers shown on the IGM maps were completely bare of snow. Examples include Iliniza Norte and Sincholagua. It is possible that more snow and ice will be found on these peaks in the mid 1980s, after the wet years 1982/3.

Not only is there variation in the climate from year to year, but the daily weather is also highly unpredictable. There is a local saying that in the mountains all four seasons can be experienced in one day. As Michaux notes in his *Ecuador: A Travel Journal* (1928)

"Morning summer.
Noon springtime. The sky is beginning to get overcast.
4 p.m. rain. Freshness.
A night cold and luminous like winter.
For this reason clothing is a problem if you must be out for more than a few hours.
You watch the accursed setting forth, armed with straw hat, canvas, furpiece, and umbrella."

It is amazing and confusing that so much variation can be found in such a small area. One can sum up by saying that December to January are the best months to be in the Ecuadorian mountains and

March to May the worst. If you're there in June through September, avoid the east and climb in the west. In October through February concentrate on the east. Cotopaxi lies in a strange dry micro-climate of its own and can be climbed during most of the year.

MOUNTAINEERING – A HISTORICAL VIEW

Despite some legends there is no evidence, as found in the more southerly countries, of any mountain ascents by the local Indians prior to the arrival of the Spanish *conquistadores* who contented themselves with noting major volcanic activity in their journals, their first records being of the eruptions of Cotopaxi and Tungurahua in 1534. The earliest recorded ascent is that of the Ecuadorian* José Toribio Ortiguera who reached the crater of Pichincha in 1582. There is a disputed record of an ascent of Pichincha by Padre Juan Romero in 1660, the same year that a major eruption buried Quito in 40 cm of volcanic ash, but generally speaking during the first two centuries of Spanish occupation there was little interest in geographical aspects. The windfall of a treasure-laden Inca civilization was something the Spaniards wished to exploit themselves and so all foreign visitors, including natural historians or explorers, were regarded with suspicion. It was not until well into the eighteenth century that a European scientific expedition was first permitted to make a serious attempt at mapping and exploring Ecuador and this led to an awakening of interest in the mountains of the country.

By the beginning of the eighteenth century it had been established that the world was round, but controversy still raged over the concept of polar flattening. In an attempt to settle the issue, the French Académie des Sciences organized expeditions to the arctic and the equator. At this time Africa was still the 'dark continent', Indonesia was little known, and the Amazon basin virtually unexplored. Consequently Ecuador, with its capital just 25 km south of the equator, was the obvious venue for such an expedition. This took place from 1736 to 1744 and was led by the Frenchman Charles-Marie de La Condamine, accompanied by two countrymen, two Spaniards, and an Ecuadorian. Surveying was undertaken, and their calculations of the length of the equator became the basis of the metric system of weights and measures. The flora, fauna, geology, and geography were also studied. The explorers were very interested in the highlands, and during the course of their investigations concluded that Chimborazo (6310 m) was the highest peak in the world – a belief which existed until the 1820s. They made the first serious attempt to scale this mountain, reaching an altitude of about 4750 m.

*Note: I use 'Ecuadorian' for convenience here and later in the chapter although the country was not known by that name until 1830.

The less important peaks of Pichincha (4794 m) and Corazón (4788 m) were successfully climbed and most of the major peaks were surveyed. This expedition's surveys and measurements started a series of disputes which have not been resolved to this day. For example Cotopaxi, Ecuador's second highest peak, was measured at 5751 m by La Condamine's expedition. Succeeding expeditions turned in considerably higher measurements: 5753 m by Humboldt in 1802, 5978 m by Whymper in 1880, 5940 m by Martínez in 1906, and the highest of all, 6005 m was published by Arthur Eichler in his *Ecuador – Snow Peaks and Jungles* (1970). His is the only figure of over 6000 m and the height most generally accepted today is 5897 m as surveyed by the Instituto Geográfico Militar in 1972. Nevertheless many recent sources are still unable to agree on the correct elevation. The same perplexing situation exists with other peaks (see *Appendix*).

After the departure of the French expedition, the eighteenth century saw no more major exploration of the Ecuadorian mountains. It was not until 1802 that an expedition led by the famous German scientist and explorer Baron Alexander von Humboldt reawakened interest in the Ecuadorian highlands. Humboldt visited and studied various peaks including Cotopaxi, Pichincha, Antisana, and El Altar but it is for his research on and attempted ascent of Chimborazo that his expedition is particularly remembered by mountaineers. Accompanied by the Frenchman Aimé Bonpland and the Ecuadorian Carlos Montúfar he identified many plants including some new species, as well as noting barometric data during his attempted ascent of the southern flanks of the mountain. He made a sectional sketch map of Chimborazo which shows the plant species, various geographical landmarks, the expedition's penetration beyond the snowline and finally, high above the surrounding *páramo* the comment, "Crevasse qui empêcha les voyageurs d'attendre la cime" (crevasse which prevents travellers from reaching the summit). This indicates the point at about 5875 m where Humboldt and his companions, suffering from high altitude sickness, with cracked and bleeding lips and badly sun-burned faces, were forced to turn back. This attempt is particularly noteworthy since despite their failure to gain the summit, they did reach the highest point so far attained by western man.

Since Chimborazo was still considered the highest mountain in the world, other attempts on its summit soon followed. The Venezuelan liberator of the Andean countries, Simón Bolívar, climbed to the snowline in 1822 and nine years later Bolívar's colonel, the French agronomist Joseph Boussingault, managed to reach about 6000 m on Chimborazo's southern slopes, again increasing the altitude so far attained by western explorers. Boussingault also made several attempts on other peaks, but without notable success.

President Gabriel García Moreno, a much criticized and despotic ruler, was nevertheless the first Ecuadorian leader to take an active interest in the environment. He enacted several conservationist laws and in 1844 climbed to the crater of Pichincha. In succeeding years several European expeditions arrived. Around 1847 the almost forgotten Italian traveller Gaetano Osculati spent a year in Ecuador, and although he made no attempts to climb any of its peaks he left us with some interesting paintings and drawings of Ecuadorian mountains. 1849 saw the first recorded expedition to the highly active volcano Sangay (5230 m) where the Frenchman Sebastian Wisse counted 267 strong explosions in one hour. During the 1850s and 1860s several expeditions from various nations visited Ecuador but achieved little, and it was not until 1872 that the next major breakthrough in Ecuadorian mountaineering occurred.

In this year the German Wilhelm Reiss, accompanied by the Colombian Angel M. Escobar, succeeded in reaching the 5897 m summit of Cotopaxi climbing the southeastern flank, rather than the northern route which has since become accepted as the normal route. The following year another German, Alfonso Stübel, accompanied by four Ecuadorians, Eusebio Rodriguez, Melchor Páez, Vicente Ramón, and Rafael Jantui reached the summit via the same route: the first major peak to have been climbed by Ecuadorians. The two Germans then joined forces and in 1873 made the first ascent of the active volcano Tungurahua (5016 m) as well as attempts on other summits.

A disastrous volcanic eruption on June 26 1877 left the slopes of Cotopaxi bare of ice and snow, and several climbers took advantage of this situation and climbed the volcano by the northeast side. Then a remarkable expedition in 1880, led by the renowned English climber Edward Whymper, succeeded in reaching the summit and spending a night by Cotopaxi's crater. Whymper had already established his reputation as a climber by making the first ascent of the Matterhorn, at one time reputed to be impossible. His Ecuadorian expedition must surely rate as one of the most successful mountaineering expeditions ever undertaken. With the Italian cousins Louis and Jean-Antoine Carrel, Whymper proceeded to climb not only Cotopaxi but also made the first ascent of Chimborazo, a climb which raised a storm of disbelief and protest. To quell his critics Whymper repeated the climb later in 1880 accompanied by two Ecuadorians, David Beltrán and Francisco Campaña. Ecuador's third highest peak, Cayambe (5790 m), and Antisana (5704 m), the fourth highest, also fell to the ice axes of Whymper and the Carrels as did Iliniza Sur (5263 m), Carihuairazo (5020 m), Sincholagua (4893 m), Cotacachi (4939 m) and Sara Urco (4676 m). In addition to these eight first ascents several other climbs were made by this expedition including Corazón and Pichincha as well as an unsuccessful attempt on El Altar (5319 m) which is Ecuador's most technical snow peak and which was not climbed until 1963. Edward Whymper is remembered in Ecuador to this day; there is a street named after him in

Quito and the country's highest mountaineers' refuge, the new and well equipped hut at 5000 m on Chimborazo's eastern slopes, has been named Refugio Whymper.

After Whymper's memorable exploits no important expeditions occurred until the twentieth century. Whereas the nineteenth century had seen many important European expeditions to the Ecuadorian Andes, the twentieth century saw an awakening of interest in mountaineering by national climbers. The father of Ecuadorian mountaineering is Nicolás Martínez who in the first decades of this century succeeded in making many notable ascents. In 1900 Martínez climbed Tungurahua (5016 m), and in succeeding years climbed this peak several more times. His interest in mountaineering awakened, Martínez made first Ecuadorian ascents of many major peaks: Antisana in 1904, a failed attempt on Cayambe in 1905, and successful climbs of Cotopaxi and Chimborazo in 1906. Succeeding years saw various successes and failures in Martínez's climbing career. A particularly noteworthy ascent was that of Iliniza Norte in 1912; this 5126 m peak is the only one of Ecuador's ten 5000 m peaks which was first climbed by an Ecuadorian.

The first world war and its aftermath left little time or money for new foreign expeditions to Ecuador and it was not until 1929 that a United States expedition, led by Robert T. Moore, achieved the first ascent of Sangay (5230 m). This, the most continuously active volcano in Latin America, was experiencing a rare period of tranquillity at the time. Moore's expedition also made various other notable climbs, including the first US ascent of Chimborazo.

By 1929 all but one of the major Ecuadorian peaks (the ten 5000 m ones) had been conquered. The exception was El Altar (5319 m) Ecuador's fifth highest peak which was not climbed until 1963 when an Italian Alpine Club expedition led by Marino Tremonti succeeded in reaching the summit. In the intervening years many repeat ascents of the major peaks were made by climbers of all nationalities and various minor peaks were conquered for the first time. These included Cerro Hermoso (4571 m) by four Germans in 1941 and Quilindaña (4878 m) by a large party of Ecuadorians, Colombians, French, and Italians in 1952.

The 1960s and 1970s saw a new approach to mountaineering in Ecuador. With Tremonti's first ascent of El Altar in 1963 all the major peaks had been climbed and emphasis was laid on climbing new routes and lower summits of the more important mountains. El Altar's eight other virgin peaks provided great impetus and excitement to Ecuadorian mountaineering as, one by one, they were climbed between 1965 and 1979 by climbers of various nationalities, including three first ascents by Ecuadorian climbers. During these decades Ecuadorian mountaineers were consistently in the forefront of finding new climbs, such as the second and third summits of Antisana, new routes on Cayambe and Iliniza Sur, the Central Summit on Chimborazo, the first ascents of the minor peaks of Achipungo and

Ayapungo, and many others too numerous to mention. In connection with these new climbs the names of the Ecuadorians Joseph Bergé, Marco Cruz, James Desrossiers, Milton Moreno, Ramiro Navarrete, Romulo Pazmiño, the Reinoso brothers, Santiago Rivadeneira, and Iván Rojas will be long remembered. Many of these and other Ecuadorian climbers have also made notable ascents in different parts of the world. Mention should also be made of Fabián Zurita who, perhaps more than any other Ecuadorian, has brought the mountains of Ecuador closer to its people through his frequent and non-technical articles in the Ecuadorian press.

In the 1960s it was realized that mountaineering in Ecuador was economically important as a tourist asset and refuges were constructed to accommodate visiting foreign as well as national climbers. The first of these was the now badly damaged Fabián Zurita refuge built in 1964 at 4900 m on the northwest slopes of Chimborazo. Since then seven more mountain huts have been built; some are extremely basic and others very comfortable.

Today, with its network of climbing huts and their easy accessibility, Ecuador has become an important mountaineering centre. For professionals and experts it still provides the opportunity for good new routes but it is of particular interest to intermediate climbers who wish to experience the excitement of high altitude ascents. It is also very useful as a high altitude training ground for climbers wishing to test and improve their skills before attempting ascents in the difficult mountains of the more southern Andes.

CHAPTER 2
PREPARATIONS

GETTING THERE

From Europe there are direct flights on major airlines but these are expensive. In many major cities (particularly London, Amsterdam, Antwerp, and Zurich) there are 'bucket shops' which are unlicensed airline ticket agencies. How they work is too complicated to explain here - but they are legal and can sell you discounted tickets for as little as half the usual price. They advertise in various newspapers and magazines; in Britain try anything from *Time Out* to *The Times*. Bucket shops sell cheap tickets and nothing else - if you need travel information contact Journey Latin America (JLA) who are experts in arranging discount and youth fares for this part of the world and are pleased to answer unusual travel queries from their customers. Their address is: JLA, 10 Barley Mow Passage, London W4 4PH. Tel. 01-994 6477.

From North America there are no really inexpensive flights. Your best bet is a cheap excursion ticket from Miami. Ecuador is well placed for overland journeys from either Colombia in the north or Peru in the south so look out for cheap flights to those destinations. Bear in mind that there is a 10% tax on air tickets bought in Ecuador and a US $8 departure tax from the airport for international flights.

Finally, passenger and cargo ships call at Guayaquil from all over the world - but voyages are often more expensive than flights.

DOCUMENTS

Everyone needs a passport valid for at least 6 months and a tourist card which is valid for up to 90 days and is available from any port of entry. You are legally required to be able to show evidence of 'sufficient funds' (as much as US $20 per day) and an exit ticket from the country - but this is not always asked for, particularly if travelling overland. An MCO (Miscellaneous Charges Order) from any IATA airline is often adequate. Your tourist card is easily renewed at the Department of Immigration in Quito at Av. Amazonas 3149 and in other major cities. but tourists are allowed a maximum of only 90 days in any one calendar year. Obtaining permission for a longer stay is usually a time-consuming and frustrating process even if you have genuine reasons for extending your visit (e.g. study or business). If your 90 days have expired and you need to enter the country (to catch an international flight from Quito, for example) a 3 day transit visa can be issued.

WHAT TO BRING

In the words of Edward Whymper, "It is indeed true that nearly everything may be obtained in Ecuador. It is also true that we often had great difficulty in obtaining anything." Although climbing and backpacking equipment is available for sale and hire it is usually very expensive and often inadequate. If you're large then you'll have difficulty in finding clothing and particularly footwear to fit you since Ecuadorians are generally small. It is best to bring what you need with you. It is easy enough to find storage facilities for your excess gear whilst you are hiking or climbing.

The following checklists reflect the fact that while you may be a mountaineer one day, you'll be just a tourist the next. I've included everything I consider useful but doubtless some people's needs will differ from mine.

BACKPACK. Bear in mind that an external frame pack, while very comfortable, is awkward if hitch-hiking and liable to break during the rough treatment it will receive on planes, buses, and trucks. External frame packs tend to snag on everything from hotel doors to tropical vegetation and to throw the climber off balance; an internal frame or frameless pack hugs the body better. Buy as large a pack as you can carry – when the weather's terrible and your hands are cold it's easier to stuff a sopping wet tent and gear into a large pack than to struggle with a small one which held everything so snugly when you were warm and dry in your hotel.

SLEEPING BAG.   It gets cold – but not very cold. Even when mountaineering high above the snowline temperatures below -10°C are not very common, so you don't need the most expensive sleeping bag. A medium weight one is adequate, especially if combined with a bivouac sac (waterproof sleeping bag cover) or a down jacket. If you plan on doing a lot of backpacking then you should consider a bag with artificial filling because it will stay fairly warm when wet, whilst a soggy down bag is almost useless. At present artificial fillings are cheaper than down, though heavier and bulkier, but lighter new materials are constantly being developed.

MATTRESS. This is essential. Any closed cell (ensolite type) foam pad will do. I use a cheap light one which works as well as more expensive ones for insulation (which is the most important thing) although for comfort you may want a more elaborate one such as a Thermarest, which is a combination air mattress/foam pad.

TENT. You can manage without a tent if you climb only the major peaks as good mountain refuges are available. If planning extended hikes or climbs, however, you'll need a tent which is waterproof and withstands buffeting by high winds, although some climbers make do with bivouac sacs instead. I used a single-walled Gore-Tex tent for two years and it stayed more or less dry even in all night epic rain storms. Gore-Tex is unique in that it 'breathes' so there is less condensation problem. All tent seams must be carefully water-proofed with seam-sealer before leaving home.

STOVE. Four of Ecuador's climbers' huts have kitchens with stoves but if you plan trips away from the huts you'll need a stove as there is little firewood in the highlands. The best stove for high altitudes is the American MSR G/K which runs on white gas (*gasolina de cocina*, available from some petrol stations), paraffin (kerosene, sold as 'Kerex' in Ecuador), and even car and aviation fuel. The drawback to this excellent stove is its cost and the difficulty of obtaining it in Great Britain. In this country the best alternative is probably the Optimus 96 which burns paraffin. Another very good stove is the Bleuet Gaz 200 which operates on gas cartridges which are sometimes obtainable in Ecuador as well as in Europe and the USA. If you use this stove don't litter the mountains with 'dead' cartridges, and remember that you may not carry them on aeroplanes.

COOKING UTENSILS AND CUTLERY. Bring your own or buy them in Ecuador; the locals use cheap, lightweight pans which are available in any town. Aluminium spoons and plastic cups are also common.

WATER BOTTLE. I carry one or two light plastic 1 litre water bottles and a 2 gallon water bag (which weighs 4 oz and packs smaller than my fist) for carrying water to campsites.

LIGHT. Being on the equator means you can be sure of one thing: 12 hours of darkness. So you'll be needing light more than in the northern summers. Torches (flashlights) and batteries are available throughout Ecuador, as are candles. Slow-burning candles are particularly useful but cannot be bought in Ecuador. For large groups you can bring a lantern to fit Bleuet gaz cartridges.

FOOD. With a little imagination you can find plenty of food suitable for backpacking and climbing in Ecuador's stores. Freeze dried food is virtually unobtainable but you can use noodles, dried soups, chocolate, raisins, nuts, oatmeal, powdered juices, dried milk, cheese, crackers, biscuits, salami, cans of fish, and peanut butter.

FOOTWEAR. You can climb most peaks with heavy hiking boots although double climbing boots are warmer. Medium weight hiking boots are adequate for all the hikes and some of the lesser peaks; you'll need good Vibram soles. EBs and similar rock climbing boots with smooth rubber soles are useless. Ex-army jungle boots are the best footwear for jungle and lowland trips. Bring a pair of light shoes, sneakers, or sandals, for sitting around camp and walking in cities, and some rubber thongs (flip-flops) for use in dubious hotel bathrooms.

All footwear stops at English size 9 (43 metric) in Ecuador. This includes socks, so large people should bring spares. Heavy woollen socks are best for keeping feet warm, and cotton and nylon liners help prevent blisters.

CLOTHING.   Thermal underwear (both top and bottom) can be slept in and keeps you warm at high altitudes. Jeans are useless in the mountains as they bind on your legs when climbing and offer no insulation when wet. They are also too hot to wear in the sun, heavy to carry, hard to wash, and take ages to dry. (Despite this, they're the gringo item most frequently stolen from washing lines.) For climbers, woollen mountaineering trousers are excellent, or a pair of fibrepile trousers combined with rain pants to keep out the wind. One or two pairs of lightweight slacks are good for town and lowland use. Gaiters are useful for mountaineering.

Bring at least one light long sleeved shirt to protect against the intense tropical sun. You can buy thick woollen sweaters (even large sizes) cheaply in the Indian markets, so think twice about carrying sweaters from home. I like fibrepile pullovers or jackets which stay warm when wet, dry quickly, and are lighter than wool. Bring your usual assortment of tee shirts etc., and one warm wool shirt.

Without a doubt, a down jacket (or one with artificial filling) is the single most useful clothing item. Even if you're not planning any high altitude mountaineering it's useful for the hikes which go over 4000 m and are very cold at night.

Raingear is essential as it can rain even during the 'dry' season. Nylon ponchos are better than nothing but are a problem in the wind. A rain jacket and separate trousers are better. Gore-Tex is expensive but it works – this waterproof material allows sweat to evaporate so you don't get wet from perspiration.

A hat is essential for mountaineering and high altitude hikes. Up to 40% of your body heat can escape from your exposed head and neck so it really helps to keep warm if you wear a wool hat or better still a balaclava which also protects your face and neck. A wide brimmed sun hat is good for calm, sunny days and in the lowlands. Two pairs of gloves are needed by mountaineers: a light inner pair and a heavy wool outer mitt. Hikers will get by with one warm pair. Shorts are not worn in the towns but are comfortable for lower hikes in remote regions and for visits to coast, rivers, and hot pools. Also bring swimwear. All trousers should have deep pockets, preferably secured with buttons, zipper, or velcro (see *Security*) and they're handy in shirts (and skirts) as well. You may have to add them yourself.

MOUNTAINEERING EQUIPMENT. Ropes, ice axe, and crampons are the basic necessities for snow climbs – often you can get by with nothing else. A second tool (ice hammer) is useful for some mountains (as detailed in the text). Protection may be needed for less experienced climbers, particularly whilst descending and for crevasse rescue. Two long ice screws and two snow stakes (with their respective slings and carabiners) will normally suffice. Make prussiks in case you fall into a crevasse. A helmet is occasionally useful. A bivi sac is worth throwing into your pack just in case . . . . A mountaineers' headlamp is needed for the predawn departures which are standard features of most snow climbs. Bring one from home as Ecuadorian ones are too heavy. Alkaline batteries are available in Quito, but the new lithium batteries, which can last for 60 hours of continuous use, are not.

Glacier cream (not ordinary sun-tan lotion), lip salve, and climbers' goggles are essential – the power of the equatorial sun bouncing off glaciers at 6000 m will astound you. A friend of mine became snow blind while wearing ordinary sun-glasses.

Footpaths in Ecuador are not signposted or marked in any way, so a compass is essential for following my directions particularly when hiking cross-country. Bring marker flags or wands (which can be made from sticks and strips of plastic from plastic bags). Gaiters and good climbers' gloves should be packed. Other useful but not essential items are ski poles, an altimeter, and a climbers' harness.

MISCELLANEOUS USEFUL ITEMS. Pocket torch (flashlight) with spare bulbs and batteries; travel alarm clock; Swiss Army style penknife; sewing kit (including large needles and thick thread for heavy repairs); scissors; a few metres of cord (for clotheslines, emergency repairs, spare shoelaces, tent guys, etc.); spare glasses; sun-glasses; binoculars; camera; plenty of film. A compass is more than useful, it is essential.

Plastic bags (including large trash bin liners to cover packs at night); flat rubber universal bath plug; soap for clothes and body (in a soap dish); shampoo; tooth brush and paste, and dental floss (great for emergency repairs); towel; toilet paper (rarely found in cheaper hotel and restaurant lavatories); ear plugs for noisy hotels and buses; insect repellant; sun-tan lotion; hand-cream.

Pens and pencils; address book; notebook for journal and letter writing; paperback book (easily exchanged with other travellers when you've finished); pocket Spanish–English dictionary; waterproof matches or cigarette lighter; waterproofing for boots; small padlock (for cheap hotel rooms or locking gear in storage); a large lightweight nylon bag for leaving gear in storage; medicine kit (see *Health* section).

MONEY MATTERS

The Ecuadorian currency is the sucre, divided into a hundred centavos. At the time of writing (1983) the rate of exchange was 90 sucres to the US dollar and its value was fluctuating weekly with a slow downward trend.

The pound sterling, the German mark, and the French or Swiss franc can normally be changed in Quito but the US dollar is the most readily accepted currency, especially outside the capital. There is normally little difference in exchange rates between dollar travellers cheques and cash. There are slight variations in exchange rates between different banks and *casas de cambio* (exchange houses) so it pays to shop around if exchanging a lot of money. Rodrigo Paz, a *casa de cambio* which has several branches including the main one at Amazonas 370 in Quito, usually gives a good rate. Exchange facilities are available at the airport seven days a week or try the Hotel Colón. There is no black market.

Travellers cheques are the most convenient and safe way of carrying large amounts of money. Guard against robbery by dividing your travellers cheques and keeping them in different places, and be conscientious about recording each cheque cashed so that if the worst happens you can get a quick refund. Be careful which travellers cheques you buy. American Express are recommended; in the event of loss or theft refunds can normally be arranged within 48 hours if you report the loss promptly and back up your claim with a police report (easily obtained), the receipts to show you paid for the cheques, and personal identification (passport). Other companies are less efficient. I had about US $400 in travellers cheques stolen over a year ago; half were American Express and were replaced in 3 days, but I am still waiting to receive my money from First National City Bank. So don't use the latter.

If you run out of money it is relatively simple to have more sent from home. Unlike most Latin American countries, Ecuador will pay you all your money in US dollars. All you need to do is pick a Quito bank which will co-operate with your bank at home (e.g. Bank of America, Bank of London and South America) and ask your family or bank manager to deposit the money in your name in the Ecuadorian bank you have chosen; if you use the telex your money can arrive in 72 hours if there are no hitches or holidays.

BUDGETING. With the recent devaluation of the sucre Ecuador has become one of the cheapest countries in Latin America for visitors with hard currency. As long as this situation prevails you could manage on the classic bare bones budget of US $5 per day. Buses running from the Colombian border to the Peruvian border cost the ridiculously low total of about US $10 for the 1000 km journey. Basic hotels charge only about a dollar a night, and there's usually a good selection of more comfortable ones that are still very economical.

If you're broke and desperate (I've been down to my last US $50 in the world a few times in South America), don't give up. You can always sell your climbing and backpacking gear easily. Good quality equipment is difficult to find in Ecuador and imported items are heavily taxed so local climbers like to buy North American or European gear from penniless mountaineers. The same applies to your camera or cassette recorder or whatever. Used but good equipment can often be sold for its original price – even more if you're a shrewd businessman or a smooth hustler, depending on your point of view. A good place to advertise is the well known budget hotel, the Gran Casino (see *Accommodation* in Chapter 3). You can also approach climbers you meet on the mountains or go to climbing clubs. Another way of making money is by teaching English. This will at least leave your weekends free to hike and climb, and you'll still have the gear to do it with. There are several language schools and the turnover is high – again the Gran Casino is a good place to look for contacts. You don't need experience, just act schoolteacherish!

INSURANCE

Carrying Amex travellers cheques insures your money but you should get comprehensive travel insurance against theft, accidents, and illness. Most travel agents will advise you of available policies but shop around and read the small print carefully. Often you'll find that certain activities, including mountaineering, aren't covered. In the UK, the British Mountaineering Council can supply a comprehensive and not too expensive climbers' insurance policy. This is available to members only. Write to the BMC Insurance Department, Crawford House, Precinct Centre, Booth St East, Manchester M13 9R2, and ask for Expedition Remote Area forms. The insurance company, after hearing your plans, will offer a policy to suit your needs.

In addition to hospital coverage, you should consider a policy which includes evacuation to your home country if you become seriously ill or injured.

PHOTOGRAPHY

This is worth thinking about before you go. Cameras are expensive in Ecuador so bring everything you'll need. Film is not very cheap, but less expensive than in most Latin American countries. The choice of film is limited and my personal favourite, Kodachrome 64, is not available in Ecuador. (If you're hoping to publish anything on your return, remember that some magazine editors won't consider anything but Kodachrome.) Slide films which are available are Ektachrome, Fujichrome, and Agfachrome. High speed Ektachrome 400 is good for the jungle, which is always darker than you'd expect. Kodacolor print film and most black and white film is easily found but always check the expiry date; I've seen professional looking camera stores selling film which is 2 years out of date. Film processing is sometimes shoddy and Kodachrome cannot be developed in Ecuador.

Shadows in the tropics are very dark and come out almost black in photographs. A bright cloudy day is therefore often better for photography than a very sunny one. Taking shots in open shade or using fill-in flash will help. The best time for photography is when the sun is low: the first two hours after dawn and the last two before sunset. At high altitudes a haze can spoil your pictures; using a UV filter will improve them.

The people of Ecuador are both picturesque and varied. From the handsomely uniformed presidential guard to a charmingly grubby smiling Indian child – the possibilities of 'people pictures' are endless. However, most people resent having a camera thrust into their faces without so much as a 'by your leave'. Indians in markets will often proudly turn their backs on pushy photographers. You should ask for permission with a smile or a joke, and if this is refused don't become offended. Some people are fed up at seeing their pictures in magazines or on postcards – they realize that someone must be making money at their expense. Others are still superstitious about bad luck being brought on them by cameras. Carrying a cheap polaroid is one way of gaining people's confidence – you can give them one photo whilst shooting more for yourself with your better camera. Sometimes a 'tip' is asked for. Taking photos from a discreet distance with a telephoto lens is another possibility. Be aware and sensitive of people's feelings; it is never worth upsetting someone for a good photograph.

HEALTH

BEFORE YOU GO.   Though not required by law, normal precautions for tropical travel should be taken. Vaccinations against typhoid, tetanus, and poliomyelitis are strongly advised, as is a yellow fever immunisation if you are visiting the Oriente. A cholera inoculation is only necessary if an epidemic has been declared anywhere in the world. Smallpox has been eradicated worldwide and inoculations are no longer required.

A full course of the necessary inoculations with boosters can take 6 weeks or more so be sure to see your doctor well before departure. Carry, and keep up to date, your international vaccination card.

Another inoculation to consider is gamma globulin which is fairly effective against hepatitis. The only real cure for this debilitating liver disease is a couple of months complete rest in bed. Hepatitis is caused by ingesting contaminated food or water; salads, uncooked or unpeeled fruit, unboiled drinks, and dirty syringes (even in hospitals) are the worst offenders. Infection risks are minimized by using bottled drinks, washing your own salads with purified water, and paying scrupulous attention to your toilet habits. Gamma globulin shots should be repeated every 6 months, although some authorities recommend more frequent shots. Constant research is being carried out to combat this disease and it is expected that more effective prophylaxis will be available within the next few years.

If you're planning a visit to a lowland area anti-malaria pills are recommended since the disease is on the increase in Latin America. If you stay above 2500 m you aren't at risk since mosquitoes don't live this high. Pills must be taken from 2 weeks before you enter a malaria area until 6 weeks after you leave. Check the dose carefully as it varies with the brand. You can also avoid getting bitten by always wearing long sleeved shirts and long trousers, using frequent applications of insect repellant, and sleeping under a mosquito net. If you buy insect repellant remember that the active ingredient is diethyl-metatoluamide. Some repellants contain less than 10% of this and others over 90%, so check the composition of the repellant before you buy. I find that the rub-on lotions are the most effective, and the sprays are useful for your clothes.

Finally, think about your physical condition. If you are planning a short, intensive trip and hope to climb several major peaks you should carry out regular pre-departure exercises such as swimming, running, cycling or whatever you prefer. If planning a longer trip then doing some of the Quito area day hikes will help get you into shape.

IN ECUADOR. The drastic change of diet you will experience during your stay means you'll probably be sick at least once. Stomach upsets are almost unavoidable but this is nothing to worry about. Diarrhoea is the most common ailment; drink plenty of fluids, rest, and fast, and the condition will normally clear up in about 24 hours. Symptoms and remedies for other travellers' maladies are easily found elsewhere, so I am concentrating on the more specialized area of mountain health. If you get very sick, see a doctor. Many Ecuadorian doctors speak English, have been educated in the US, and are very good. Your embassy or hotel can recommend one.

MOUNTAIN HEALTH

Hiking and climbing in the Ecuadorian countryside is more likely to keep you healthy than to make you ill. However conditions can be extreme and perhaps disastrous for the uninitiated. The major medical problems you may be faced with can be classed in four groups: those caused by cold, heat, altitude, and injury. This section is designed to help you recognize and deal with these problems.

HYPOTHERMIA. Often known as 'exposure', this insidious killer occurs when the body loses heat faster than it can produce it. Medically it exists when rectal temperature falls below 35°C or 95°F. Heat loss leading to hypothermia often occurs when the temperature is well above freezing, and is caused primarily by wet clothing and by the removal of body heat by the wind, especially from the head and neck which can lose up to 40% of body heat.

Prevention is better than cure. Put on rain gear as soon as it begins to rain and not after you're soaking wet. Wear several layers of clothing which can be removed to regulate your temperature; one very thick layer may cause you to get wet through perspiration. If you do get wet remember to wear a windproof layer; at least your wet clothes will stay a little warmer. Cotton clothes (e.g. jeans) lose 90% of their insulating properties when wet, whilst wool only loses 50%. Artificial fibrepile is also a good wet insulator and has the added advantage of drying much more quickly than wool. Remember to keep your head and neck warm. Exposed hands should be covered – use spare socks in an emergency.

If you take the above precautions you are unlikely to get hypothermia but lack of judgement or an accident can soon change a normal situation into a dangerous one. The hypothermia victim will begin feeling tired and start shivering uncontrollably. At this stage one can still stop hypothermia by getting out of the wind and rain and wearing more dry clothes (camping, getting into a dry sleeping bag, and eating some warm food). If this is not done, the person affected will begin to lose co-ordination, have difficulty in speaking, and show a lack of judgement. By this stage the victim is in serious trouble as he can't get warm himself and must be rewarmed by his friends. Climbing into a cold sleeping bag is inadequate as the victim won't have enough body heat to warm the bag. The bag must be warmed. The best way is for someone to share his sleeping bag after first removing wet clothing. If you're alone then try to make a hot water bottle with your canteen and drink small quantities of warm liquids. The final stage of hypothermia is a lapse into irrationality and incoherence, with hallucinations and disorientation, and a slow irregular pulse. The skin becomes blue and cold, and drowsiness and dilation of the pupils follow. Then come unconsciousness and death. The whole process can take *as little as two hours!* The combination of cold, wet, and windy weather is common in the Ecuadorian highlands, so be prepared; even on a day hike carry hat, gloves, wind and rain jacket, and a spare warm sweater.

FROSTBITE. This occurs when any part of the body becomes frozen. Backpackers are less likely to experience it but snow and ice climbers are possible candidates. The usual ways of getting frostbite are by exposing or wetting skin or by cutting off blood circulation to the extremities. These problems can be avoided by always wearing gloves and balaclava helmet in extremely cold conditions. The nose and cheeks are more difficult to protect. A scarf or handkerchief wrapped bandit style around the face will help, as will rewarming your nose with your hand at frequent intervals. (Rubbing snow onto the area, the traditional 'cure', is actually dangerous.) Ensure good blood circulation in your feet by not lacing boots and crampon straps too tightly. Keep your socks dry and unwrinkled. Bear in mind that exposed flesh will freeze more rapidly in windy conditions (the 'wind chill factor').

Some people are more susceptible to frostbite than others. Frostbite is liable to recur in those areas of the body which have been previously frozen. Smokers are more susceptible as are people weakened by hypothermia, exhaustion, drugs, injury, or blood loss.

The first symptom is pain. Warm and protect the area with extra clothing or by putting in a warm place (e.g. warm your face with your hands or put your hands in your groin). Restore circulation to your feet by stamping them and loosening your laces. The pain may often increase in intensity during the first minutes of rewarming but this will soon disappear. If the pain disappears without rewarming and numbness takes its place, then the problem is getting serious. The area becomes whitish and hard. Even at this late stage a small frostbitten area can be rewarmed without damage. If your feet are involved then ask a friend to warm them on his belly or in his armpit.

If a whole finger or toe (or larger area) becomes deeply frostbitten then the situation is grave. This is because rewarming the part will cause it to become extremely delicate and sensitive so it cannot be used at all for several weeks. For this reason a badly frostbitten climber should be taken to hospital to be rewarmed. Once a part has been frostbitten it can remain that way for several days without much more damage and so a climber with severe frostbite should be evacuated under his own steam as soon as possible. This is entirely feasible in Ecuador as most climbing areas are within a couple of days of Quito. Once in hospital, a badly frostbitten area must be gently thawed in water just above blood temperature or damage will result.

HEAT EXHAUSTION. A calm, sunny day in the high Andes can be extremely hot and heat problems are not uncommon, although they are more of a danger on lowland hikes. Lack of liquids aggravates this condition so drink as much as possible before setting off on a hike or climb. If you are unusually tired, thirsty, giddy, suffer from cramps, and are not urinating much, you're probably suffering from heat exhaustion. Rest in the shade and drink as much as you can. Salt pills help (but only with plenty of liquid). Refrain from activity till you recover.

If symptoms of heat exhaustion are ignored, more serious problems such as heat syncope and heat stroke could develop. Therefore these warnings must be taken seriously. Ensure a high fluid intake and wear a wide brimmed sun hat and loose light clothes.

SUNBURN. This is a major problem for climbers on snow or ice because they are unaware of the power of the equatorial sun at 6000 m. The sun will reflect from the glacier and burn in all sorts of surprising places such as behind the ears, under the chin, and in the nostrils. These areas are very sensitive and must be carefully covered with glacier cream or sun block. Lip salve is needed to prevent cracked and bleeding lips. Ordinary sun-tan lotion is helpful but normally doesn't offer enough protection for climbers on a glacier. A sun protection factor of at least 10 should be used. When making a pre-dawn departure remember to stop when the sun rises and put cream on. Reapply frequently. Good glacier cream is very difficult to find in Ecuador; if you run out try zinc oxide which is more readily available. Don't be fooled by a cloud layer; the ultraviolet rays of the sun will burn you anyway. Wear a wide brimmed hat when possible. Backpackers should also be aware of sunburn and use plenty of sun-tan lotion, especially at the beginning of a trip.

SNOW BLINDNESS. The only cure for this is to have your eyes completely covered for a few days – obviously inconvenient at the top of a mountain! Snow and ice climbers must use the darkest goggles available as ordinary sunglasses are inadequate.

HIGH ALTITUDE SICKNESS. Until the 1960s this unpleasant and often dangerous reaction to high altitude was medically unknown and climbers suffering (and dying) from it were said to be suffering from pneumonia. Recent studies have shown this not to be the case and today high altitude sickness is recognized as a major mountaineering problem and studies are continuing to increase our knowledge of this condition.

It is known that high altitude sickness can be divided into three categories: Acute Mountain Sickness (AMS), Pulmonary Oedema, and Cerebral Oedema. All three are caused not just by the lack of oxygen at high altitude, but by a too rapid ascent to these heights. The best prevention is acclimatization which means not climbing too high too fast. It is unusual for anyone to be seriously affected at elevations around 2850 m (Quito's), so using Quito as a base for acclimatization is recommended. Spending about a week at this altitude is normally adequate acclimatization for climbing high.

Research has shown that an ascent of about 300–500 m per day is normally slow enough to prevent problems, but it is impractical to spend over a week climbing Chimborazo which at 6310 m is almost 3500 m above Quito. Once acclimatized in Quito, it is quite common for one day ascents to be made with little danger. Remember that high altitude sickness usually takes from 6 to 36 hours to reveal itself and so a quick ascent and descent can normally be made with few ill effects. The old maxim " Climb high and sleep low" is a good one.

Despite these reassurances, one should bear in mind that cases of high altitude sickness can occur even if precautions are taken. Every mountaineer should be able to recognize these symptoms and know how they must be dealt with.

Acute Mountain Sickness *(soroche)* is the most common of the three variations. The symptoms are severe headache, shortness of breath, nausea, vomiting, fatigue, insomnia, loss of appetite, and a rapid pulse. Irregular (Cheyne-Stokes) breathing during sleep affects some people but is relatively harmless, although disturbing to both the sleeper and his companions. The best treatment is rest and deep breathing. Analgesics may alleviate the headache (some doctors recommend non-aspirin based ones) and an adequate fluid intake must be maintained. Oxygen helps greatly and if a victim doesn't improve then a descent is called for. A climber should never force him or herself to ascend when symptoms of AMS are present as the conditions will probably worsen.

Acetazolamide or Diamox (a mild diuretic) taken for several days before the ascent may help prevent an attack of AMS. Climbers who are short on time to acclimatize should talk with their doctor about the drug. Despite encouraging reports from several recent expeditions, it should be stressed that this drug is still not completely accepted in medical circles. Apart from the annoyance of frequent urination, other possible adverse reactions include increased cold sensitivity, numbness, and tingling in the extremities.

Pulmonary Oedema kills climbers in South America each year. It is a more extreme form of AMS and in addition to the symptoms mentioned the victim suffers from increased shortness of breath when at rest and a dry, rattling cough. As the condition worsens, frothy, bloodstained sputum is produced and the victim turns blue. Fluid collects in the lungs, literally drowning the person if his condition is not recognized. He must immediately be assisted to a lower altitude (at least 600 m lower) and taken to hospital if necessary.

Cerebral Oedema is less common but equally dangerous. Here the fluid accumulates in the brain instead of the lungs and may cause permanent brain damage or death. Symptoms include an agonizing headache, giddiness, confusion, and hallucinations. Anyone showing these signs must immediately be assisted to a lower altitude. Poor judgement is also one of the symptoms so strong persuasion may have to be used to evacuate the victim.

Finally, remember that not everyone is prone to AMS and that youth and fitness make no difference. It is important for the less affected members of a climbing party to keep their eyes on climbers who may be trying to push themselves beyond sensible limits. Climbers are often so determined to reach a summit that they can jeopardize the whole expedition by trying to cover up an attack of AMS. Being affected by high altitude sickness is not a sign of inherent weakness. It often takes more courage to stop, rest, and acclimatize further than it does to keep pushing dangerously close to an attack of pulmonary oedema.

ACCIDENTS. These can vary from a simple twisted ankle on a hiking trail to multiple injuries caused by a major climbing fall. The most important advice here is never to hike or climb alone.

If a person is injured on a trail or route which is frequently travelled then it is best to wait for help or rescue. The partner should stay with the victim and ensure that he is as warm, comfortable, and reassured as possible. If you are climbing an unusual route or hiking cross-country then waiting for help may be pointless. If the partner goes for help he must make sure that he will be able to find the victim again – leave wands or markers and arrange a whistle or flashlight signal if the victim is conscious. Don't leave him alone unless it is totally unavoidable.

All climbers should carry a booklet on the principles of first-aid, particularly with reference to mountaineering injuries. The value of a course in first aid cannot be over-emphasized.

WATER PURIFICATION. Since many diseases are caught by drinking contaminated water, it is very important to sterilize your drinking supply. The simplest effective method is boiling for 20 minutes but this is both time consuming and uses a great deal of the precious fuel you've carried. Various water purifying tablets are available but they aren't wholly effective against everything: heptatitis, for instance. The most effective method is using a saturated iodine solution. Take a small (1 oz) glass bottle and put about 2-3 mm of iodine crystals in it (both iodine crystals and suitable bottles can be obtained from pharmacies). Fill the bottle with water and give it a good shake for about a minute, then let the crystals settle to the bottom. The resulting saturated solution is added to a litre of water and left for 15 minutes to produce clean drinking water. The advantage of this method is that the crystals can be used and reused hundreds of times; very little of the crystals actually dissolves and you pour only the iodine liquid into the water and leave the crystals in the 1 oz bottle for reuse. This is more effective than water purifying tablets and doesn't taste as bad. The only danger is for people who have been treated for thyroid problems and for pregnant women (whose ingestion of iodine may cause thyroid problems in their babies). Otherwise this is a safe and recommended method.

MEDICAL KIT. Assuming there is no doctor in your party, the following basic first-aid kit is suggested.

Antiseptic cream, aspirin and more powerful analgesics, Lomotil for diarrhoea, ampicillin and tetracycline antibiotics, throat lozenges, ear and eye drops, antacid tablets, travel sickness pills, alcohol swabs, water purifier, vaseline (useful for cracked or chapped skin), lip salve, foot powder.

Thermometer in a case, surgical tape, assorted sticky-plasters (band-aids), moleskin (for blisters), gauze, bandages, butterfly closures, scissors, first-aid booklet.

Sleeping pills are useful at high altitudes where inability to sleep at night is often a problem. Drugs such as Valium should be used with caution, however. Koerner reports a case of a climber sleep-walking into a crevasse after taking Valium.

Remember that some people are allergic to even simple drugs like penicillin.

HELP: Can you help us or can we help you? We need feedback for the next edition of this book, and we'd be happy to answer any questions about climbing and hiking in Ecuador providing you send a stamped addressed envelope. Write to Rob Rachowiecki, c/o Bradt Enterprises, 41 Nortoft Rd, Chalfont St Peter, Bucks SL9 0LA, England.

CHAPTER 3
IN ECUADOR

ARRIVAL

Most visitors will fly into Quito International Airport. This is about 7 km from the new city or 10 km from the old section. Taxis into town are cheap and will charge about US $2. It is normal to agree on the price beforehand. Drivers will accept cash US dollars but the airport bank is usually open for incoming international flights. If you're really broke, take a bus southbound (to your left) from outside the airport to the old town.

ACCOMMODATION

The best first class hotel in town is the Colón at Avenida Amazonas and Patria. A good middle range hotel is the Embajador at 9 de Octubre 1046 and Colón. There are many more listed in *The South American Handbook* or other guide books. Hotels and hostels tend to come in all price ranges. Family run hotels known as *pensiónes* or *residenciales* are usually good and economical.

One hotel in particular deserves special mention. This is the Gran Casino (sometimes known as the 'Gran Gringo') at García Moreno 330 and Ambato in the old town. This is one of the best known budget hotels in Latin America. It has simple rooms providing from one to six beds at just over a dollar (US) per night. There is an inexpensive restaurant open from 7 a.m. to 10 p.m. Hot water is available in the communal showers from 7 a.m. to 3 p.m. and there is also a good sauna/steam bath open all day. A one day laundry service is available (there are no self-service laundromats in Ecuador). The Gran Casino's greatest asset is the chance to meet other travellers and get the latest information on just about everything. A lot of climbers and backpackers stay here so if you're on your own it's easy to find partners. There's a message board where people advertise all sorts of gear, look for travel companions, or try to get in touch with someone. There is also a safe left luggage system. The manager,

César Gavela Jr., speaks a little English and knows a great deal about various practical aspects of Ecuadorian tourism. He is friendly and helpful and will advise you on hiring a car, doing a jungle trip, finding a mountain guide, or going to the Galapagos. Tell him I sent you!

If the simple accommodation at the Gran Casino is too basic for you, see if the Gran Casino II is open, just around the corner. It is just being finished at the time of writing and will be a comfortable mid-range hotel.

Accommodation is cheap all over Ecuador. You can always find a basic hotel for US $1 to $2 per night, and if you want something a little more luxurious than four walls and a bed you'll find plenty of reasonably priced accommodation in all the major cities.

TRANSPORTATION

Quito has a slow, crowded, but cheap bus service which covers the city thoroughly. If you're in a hurry there are many yellow taxis which charge from US $1 to $2 per ride. Settle the price before you get in – there are no meters. Taxis in other cities are a little cheaper.

A train service runs daily from Quito to Riobamba and from there to the coast at Guayaquil. There is also a daily train from Ibarra in the north to San Lorenzo on the Pacific. See Chapter 8 for more details.

The best way to travel in Ecuador is undoubtedly by bus. Quito's central bus terminal, the Terminal Terrestre, is located about 6 km south of the city on the Pan American Highway and scores of buses leave here every day to the south, east, and west. Buses heading south on the Pan American through 'The Avenue of the Volcanoes' past Latacunga, Ambato, and Riobamba are very frequent. If you can't get a direct bus to a less well known destination, take one to the nearest big town and change; the construction of central bus stations in all major Ecuadorian cities means that if you have to change buses you don't have to go looking for out of the way bus stops – all departures are from the same place.

Quito's Terminal Terrestre is a temporary affair and a brand new terminal, capable of handling well over a thousand buses a day, is under construction near Avenida Cumandá just east of the Panecillo hill in the old section. It's supposed to open in 1984.

The only section of Ecuador not served by this terminal is the north (Otavalo, Ibarra, Tulcán). Buses for these destinations are provided by several companies located in a cluster of streets under the overpass at Av. 10 de Agosto and Patria by Parque El Ejido in the new town.

Using the bus system is easy but here are some suggestions to make your journey more enjoyable. If you go to the offices in the Terminal Terrestre the day before your departure you can nearly always buy a seat in advance; this also means you can choose your seat number, and obviously the front means better views, more leg room, and a more exciting trip. With luck, you can get these front seats as late as an hour before departure; if travelling during long holiday weekends, however, everything may be sold out several days in advance, so book early.

Both small microbuses (holding twenty-two passengers) and large coaches are used. The small buses tend to be faster and more efficient.

The drivers and their assistants usually run around yelling out their destinations and looking for passengers. Often you will be on a bus going your way within a few minutes of arriving at the terminal.

Air transportation is growing in Ecuador and the main cities of Cuenca and Guayaquil have several inexpensive flights a day from Quito. Lesser cities often have daily flights. The major internal flight companies are TAME, Saeta, and SAN.

Hitch-hiking is also possible and may be the only transportation in more remote areas. Often you will be expected to pay the driver – arrange this beforehand. Free rides are more common on the major roads.

SECURITY

Rip-offs are a fact of life in Latin America, but Ecuador is safe in comparison with the worst offenders, Colombia and Peru. Nevertheless, certain precautions taken before and during the trip will make your stay a happier one.

Thieves look for easy targets. Tourists who carry a wallet or a passport in a hip pocket are asking for trouble. Leave your wallet at home; it's an easy mark for a pickpocket. Carrying a roll of paper money loosely wadded under a handkerchief in your front pocket is as safe a way as any of carrying your daily spending money. The rest should be hidden. Always use an inside pocket or (preferably) a body pouch to protect your valuables. A money belt is good; so is a neck pouch under your shirt or a leg pouch as available from the South American Explorers Club in Lima, Peru.

Bag snatching is another problem. Motorcyclists sometimes zoom past unsuspecting pedestrians and grab a shoulder bag or camera. If you put luggage down it can be stolen in seconds whilst your attention is diverted.

Crowded places are the haunts of thieves and pickpockets. A bustling market or an ill-lit bus station are prime venues for robbery so be particularly alert. Razor blades are sometimes used to slash baggage (including a pack on your back) for a grab and run raid. Don't wear expensive watches or jewellery as this also invites snatch theft.

Armed robbery is still rare in Ecuador. The area with the worst reputation is the coast, with Guayaquil being the most dangerous, particularly the south end of town near the waterfront.

I've heard recent travellers' reports of an extremely insidious form of robbery. Gringos are offered biscuits or chocolates on a bus by seemingly friendly passengers and they wake up several hours later in an alley with just a tee shirt and a pair of trousers. One person I talked to had been unconscious for two days. Unopened packages are injected with horse tranquillisers using hypodermic syringes. So . . . don't take sweets from strangers.

When travelling by public transport watch your luggage being loaded to ensure that it's not left behind, and try to keep your eye on it during stops. Don't leave valuables in vulnerable places like the easily opened outside pockets of your pack.

Beware of theft from your hotel room. Many hotels have signs that they are not responsible for theft unless valuables are placed in deposit at reception. If using cheaper hotels, you'll find you can often lock the door with your own padlock. A combination lock is more secure than a normal padlock. Some travellers carry a short length of chain for securing baggage in storage areas or on luggage racks. Camera or bag straps can be reinforced with thin chain or guitar strings to prevent slashing.

Before you leave home make a photocopy of your passport to show embassy officials should yours be stolen. Take out travellers' insurance.

When you're climbing or hiking you'll want to leave your excess luggage in a safe place. Your hotel is usually OK, but beware of other gringos claiming your luggage. Not all travellers are honest! The Gran Casino is recommended because it locks your baggage in a store room and gives you a numbered receipt – this way no one else can claim your bag. This service costs about 25 cents per bag per week.

TOURIST INFORMATION AND MAIL

The main tourist office in Quito is at Av. Reina Victoria 514 (the intersection with Roca). They are helpful for standard queries (museums, buses, restaurants, etc.).

The General Post Office is on Benalcázar at Chile. They will hold mail for you addressed Lista de Correos, Quito, Ecuador. The American Express office will also accept mail for their clients and for holders of their travellers cheques. Their postal address is Aptdo. 2605, Quito, Ecuador and their street address is Amazonas 339.

MAPS

All maps, ranging from Quito city plans to wall charts of Ecuador, are published by and available from the IGM (Instituto Geográfico Militar). Their offices and map sales department are on top of a hill on Av. T. Paz y Miño, off Av. Colombia, behind the Casa de Cultura.

There are no buses up this hill but it's not a very hard walk. A
taxi will take you for about a dollar. A permit to enter the building
is available in exchange for your passport at the main gate; it is open
from 8.00 a.m. to 3.00 p.m., Monday to Friday.

There is a single 1:1,000,000 chart of Ecuador or four sheets
making a 1:500,000 map. Most of the highlands and some of the coast
are covered by 1:50,000 topographical maps and some 1:100,000
sheets of the mountains are also available. There are 1:50,000
planametric sheets of some otherwise mapless areas. The Oriente is
largely unmapped. All extant maps are displayed in large folders so
they can be examined before buying. Topographical sheets are
available immediately but you have to wait a day for the planametric ones. A few maps of 'sensitive' areas are sold only with a
permit; this is usually obtainable from an IGM officer in the same
building. The 1:50,000 topographical maps are those useful for
hikers and climbers. A few areas have been mapped to higher scales:
1:25,000 or even 1:10,000.

The maps supplied with this book are made to complement
rather than replace the IGM sheets, so details of the sheets needed
for each hike or climb are given in the text. Many of these maps are
available from Bradt Enterprises (see page 125).

RENTING AND BUYING EQUIPMENT

There are many sports stores in Quito but the following will be
the most useful.

Yanasacha, at República 189 and Diego de Almagro, both rents
and sells climbing and camping equipment. It has a small selection
of imported gear which is heavily taxed and hence expensive. Rental
items are limited to Ecuadorian made products which may be poor
quality. A friend of mine rented some locally made crampons but the
front points bent downwards at his first attempt to climb a small ice
wall. Ecuadorian ice axes are somewhat primitive but boots and
sleeping bags are OK. For simple climbs you could get by with this
rental gear but your own is obviously better.

A good new mountaineers' store is Almacén Cotopaxi at Av. 6 de
Diciembre 1557 and Baqueadano. It is run by climbers and they
buy and sell good used equipment of all kinds. They also publish a
little climbers' magazine *Campo Abierto* and are a source of information on clubs and meetings, etc.

The sports store at Flores 220 at the corner of Plaza Santo Domingo sells fishing, snorkelling, and camping gear and is useful for
visitors to the Galapagos and Oriente.

Don't forget the notice board at the Gran Casino Hotel for buying
and selling equipment.

CLIMBING CLUBS

The International Andean Mountaineers Club, which for many years assisted gringo climbers, is now closed. The remaining clubs are all Ecuadorian and don't often organize trips for the general public. There is a certain amount of rivalry and cliquism in these Quito clubs. They are useful as centres of information but don't expect to arrive and be taken climbing the following weekend. Nuevos Horizontes meets on Tuesday and Friday evenings in an upstairs room at Venezuela 659. Sadday has evening meetings on most week-days at Manabí 621. Most of the major colleges and universities have a mountain club. The best known of these is the Colegio San Gabriel group which also irregularly publishes *Montaña* magazine. The club at the Catholic University sometimes has climbing films and lectures open to the general public. (The people at the Almacén Cotopaxi are usually in the know about forthcoming events.) There is also the Asociación de Andinismo de Chimborazo at Chile 3321 and Francia, in Riobamba.

GUIDES

This book aims to get you to the top of most mountains without a guide. Many inexperienced climbers, however, will feel more confident with one to start with.

The best known and most experienced professional guide in Ecuador is Marco Cruz who can be contacted in advance c/o Metropolitan Touring, Amazonas 239, Quito, Ecuador. He is expensive and often booked up well in advance.

In Quito you can also talk to people at the climbers' clubs and stores for recommended guides. Alan Cathey, who speaks English, German, and Spanish rarely has time to guide you himself but knows of many other climbers who will. Phone him at 241 014 or 242 855. Mathias Spatz is an enthusiastic young guide who can be reached at 241 243. He speaks English and his address is Casilla 6319, CCI, Quito, Ecuador. The manager of the Hotel Gran Casino can often put you in contact with a guide. To climb Chimborazo, talk to Sr. Enrique Veloz, president of the Asociación de Andinismo de Chimborazo in Riobamba. Phone 960 916. Other guides who work in specific areas are mentioned in the appropriate sections of the book.

Some 'guides' will drive you only as far as the climbers' refuges. Always confirm that yours will take you to the summit and has his own equipment – the latter a good indication of the guide's experience.

NATURAL HISTORY

The great variety of habitats in a country which rises from ocean to
snow peaks and drops back to tropical rainforest ensures an abun
dance of wildlife. The best known wildlife reserve is the Galapagos
Islands; the plants and animals found here are fully described in
several good guide books. The mainland, on the other hand, is a
relatively unstudied naturalist's paradise. Since there are no com
prehensive field guides to the flora and fauna, Ecuador offers wonderful opportunities for study for a field researcher but many frus-
trations for the ordinary traveller who has difficulty in identifying
this bewildering wildlife.

Although Ecuador lies in the heart of the tropics you wouldn't
call the natural history of the highlands tropical. Indeed, the vegetation here has been compared to that of the arctic tundra. This is
because altitude as well as latitude has an important influence on
the flora and fauna of an area. Pioneer work on this concept was
done in Ecuador in 1802 by the German scientist Alexander von
Humboldt. He related ecology to altitude and recognized three
major ecological zones: lowland (hot), central (temperate), and highland (cold). This last is said to begin at about 3200 m and continue
to the glaciated mountain tops. It can be sub-divided into the snow
region above about 4700 m, where insects and birds are occasionally
seen, and the area below the permanent snow line which is known as
the *páramo*.

The *páramo* is a highly specialized zone unique to tropical America,
and found only from the highlands of Costa Rica at 10°N down to
northern Peru at 10°S. Similarly elevated areas in other parts of the
world differ in their climates and evolutionary history. Most of the
hikes and climbs in this book will pass through the *páramo* and so
this section concentrates on highland ecology rather than giving space
to the overwhelmingly diverse flora and fauna of low lying areas
which deserve a book to themselves. (See *Bibliography* for suggested
further reading on the subject.)

Páramo weather is typically cold and wet, with frequent rain often
replaced by moist mists and clouds. Snow falls occasionally, and
strong winds are common. Night time temperatures are below freezing and glaring sunlight can be a hazard during short spells of fine
weather. In short, conditions are harsh, and comparatively few animals are seen. Plants, on the other hand, have adapted well to this
difficult environment and as a result the vegetation looks strange
and interesting.

The Andean flora has evolved over approximately 60 million years
of uplift of the range. Thus the vegetation has had adequate time
slowly to modify itself. The major adaptations have been the forma-
tion of smaller and thicker leaves which are less susceptible to frost;

the development of curved leaves with thick waxy skins to reflect or absorb extreme solar radiation during cloudless days; the growth of a fine hairy 'down' as insulation on the plant's surface; the arrangement of leaves into a rosette pattern to prevent them shading one another during photosynthesis and to protect the delicate centre; and the progressive compacting of the plants until they grow close to the ground where the temperature is more constant and there is protection from the wind. Thus many *páramo* plants are characteristically small and compact, some resembling a hard, waxy, green carpet. There are exceptions to this however, including the giant *frailejones* and the *puyas*.

Giant *espeletia*, locally known as *frailejones*, are a weird sight as they float into view in a typical *páramo* mist. They are high enough to resemble human beings, hence the name *frailejones* which means greyfriars. Despite their size they retain certain features of other *páramo* vegetation, such as downy hairs for insulation. *Espeletia* belong to the daisy family, and are an unmistakable feature of the northern *páramo* of Ecuador, particularly in the region of El Ángel.

Further south the *páramo* is rather drier and here we often find the *puyas*, members of the bromeliad family which replace the *frailejones* of the wetter north. The *puyas* are some of the least understood of the *páramo* plants, having very few of the normal characteristics of the plants found here. They are very large (reaching a height of over eight metres in Peru) and have no typical downy insulation. Their leaves, though still in a rosette pattern, are not small and compact but long and spiky and grow on top of a short trunk instead of at ground level.

Another attractive plant of the dry southern *páramo* is the *chuquiragua*. In some ways it resembles a tall thistle topped with orange flower heads and with stems densely covered with tough spiky leaves. This plant has medicinal properties and is used locally to soothe coughs, and for liver and kidney problems.

Apart from the flowering plants there is a great variety of other vegetation found in this zone. Everywhere you go you will encounter a spiky, resistant tussock grass which grows in clumps and makes walking rather uncomfortable. In the lower *páramo* (below 4000 m) dense thickets of small trees may be seen. These are often of the rose family and a particularly common tree is the *quinua* (*Polylepsis sp.*), locally known as *el colorado* (the red one) because its bark is a dull reddish colour. If you push your way into one of these thickets, which are common in the *páramos* of Las Cajas in the south of Ecuador, you will observe a variety of lichens, mosses, epiphytes, and fungi.

Animals have not adapted themselves quite as well as plants to this harsh environment and are never plentiful. You are most likely to see birds, toads, and rabbits.

The most exciting bird species is the Andean condor (*Vultur gryphus*). This is the largest flying bird in the world. With its three

During Whymper's visit he observed a condor hunt. A horse carcass was used to entice the birds to the ground.

metre wing span and effortless flight it is indeed magnificent – particularly from a distance. Close up, its vicious hooked beak and its uncompromisingly hard eye set in a revoltingly bare and wrinkled pink head identify it as a carrion eater. Often it soars hundreds of metres in the air and its huge size is difficult to appreciate unless there is another bird close by for comparison. It is best identified by its flat, gliding flight with 'fingered' wing tips (formed by spread primary feathers), silvery patches on the upper surface of its wings and a white neck ruff. The rest of the body is black. Condors are becoming much rarer now than in the days of Whymper, who wrote after his visit in 1880 ". . . we commonly saw a dozen on the wing at the same time." Good condor spotting areas include El Altar and Cotopaxi National Park. I even saw a pair flying over Cerro Pasochoa, just 20 km south of the capital.

Smaller birds of prey are also seen in the *páramo*. The black-chested buzzard-eagle (*Geranoaetus melanoleucus*) is quite common especially in the Papallacta area. At 58 cm in length it is one of the largest of the Ecuadorian hawks (though small compared to the 108 cm of the condor). It is identified by a very short, dark, wedge-shaped tail, a white belly finely barred with black, and blackish sides of head and breast. The throat is almost white. The most common hawk is the variable (or puna) hawk (*Buteo poecilochrous*) which is limited to the open *páramo*. 52 cm in length, its most distinctive feature is a white tail with a black band near the end. As its name suggests its plumage varies; it is usually light bellied and brown backed. The fairly small (44 cm) cinereous harrier (*Circus cinereus*) is sometimes seen. It is mostly grey with a white rump and belly barred with brown. Finally, the distinctive carunculated caracara (*Phalcobaenus carunculatus*) with its bright orange-red facial skin and legs, white belly and black above is also sighted here.

One of the most common *páramo* birds is the Andean lapwing (*Vanellus resplendens*). It is unmistakable with its harsh noisy call and its brown/white/black striped wing pattern, particularly noticeable in flight. Of the ducks, the speckled teal (*Anas flavirostris*) with its yellow bill and brown head is the most common. Lago Limpiopungo in Cotopaxi National Park is a good place for both these species, as well as the yellow-billed pintail (*Anas georgica*), the Andean gull (*Larus serranus*) and the American coot (*Fulica americana*).

If you wake up in your tent during the dark early hours of the morning to hear a weird whizzing sound like a lost UFO, don't be too alarmed. It's probably a cordillera snipe, also known as the Andean snipe (*Chubbia jamesoni*). They often fly at night and produce this strange drumming noise with their outer wing feathers. Another night flier in the *páramo* is the owl. You may catch sight of the great horned owl (*Bubo virgianus*) or even the well known barn owl (*Tyto alba*). More frequently seen is the short-eared owl

(*Asio flammeus*), because it hunts during the day.

Of the small birds found in the *páramo*, the most easily identifiable are the hummingbirds, at least 126 species of which have been listed as occurring in Ecuador alone. The Andean hillstar (*Oreotrochilus estella*) is one of the most common found at high altitudes. I've often been amazed to see one come humming past my tent at a snow line camp at 4700 m. This tiny bundle of life survives the intense night-time cold by lowering its metabolism by as much as 95% and entering an almost lifeless state, similar to hibernation. Its body temperature drops dramatically; one researcher measured a decrease from 39.5°C to 14.4°C overnight. The bird passes the night in a protected crevice or overhang and regains its day-time temperature in the morning sun with no ill effects. Hummingbirds are the smallest birds in the world and the most manoeuvrable. The Andean hillstar, at 13 cm in length, is comparatively big; the short-tailed woodstar (*Myrmia micrura*) which is common on the coast is a mere 7 cm in length and this includes the needle like bill. Their wings beat in a shallow figure of eight instead of the normal up and down; this, combined with a 'humming' 80 beats a second wingspeed enables them to hover and even fly backwards and speeds of up to 110 km per hour have been recorded.

Swallows are frequently sighted in the *páramo*; look particularly for the brown-bellied swallow (*Notiochelidon murina*) and the blue-and-white swallow (*N. cyanoleuca*); both are common. The thrushes are represented in the *páramo* by the great thrush (*Turdus fuscater*); the only pipit found is the páramo pipit (*Anthus bogotensis*). Other small species tend to come under the category of 'small brown birds'; of these the cinclodes are the easiest to recognize with a distinctive white eye stripe. The stout-billed and the bar-winged cinclodes (*C. excelsior* and *C. fuscus*) are among the commonest of all *páramo* birds.

Good places for highland ornithology are the Papallacta area and Cotopaxi National Park. Don't forget that this is a harsh environment so you won't see birds flocking in their hundreds. In the Cotopaxi park station there is a small museum which displays several dozen species of stuffed *páramo* birds; this should help you with identification.

Looking groundwards instead of skywards you'll frequently find another animal in the *páramo*: the toad. At this altitude they usually belong to the *Atelopodidae* family and are recognized by their lethargic movements and diurnal activity. They are particularly active after a heavy rain. On one walk in Cotopaxi National Park I saw literally hundreds of *Atelopus ignescens* toads almost falling over one another. They are jet black with bright orange bellies and are locally known as the jambato toad. In the more southerly *páramos* these black toads are less common and are replaced by more ordinary looking green examples of the same genus.

When talking of wildlife, it is the mammals which tend most to arouse the general observer's excitement and curiosity. Interesting and strange species live on the *páramo*, but most, unfortunately, are extremely rare and difficult to observe. The first species you will see will be rabbits (*Sylvilagus spp.*) which need no description. Semi-wild horses and cattle range in the highlands, but llamas, perhaps the animals most closely associated with the Andean mountains and their people, are found only in domestic situations. An experimental herd can be seen in Cotopaxi National Park.

Three species of deer are found in the highlands. The familiar white-tailed deer (*Odocoileus virginianus*) occurs at various altitudes and is seen fairly often in Cotopaxi National Park. Two smaller species are infrequently observed. Between 3000 and 4000 m one may see a small brocket deer (*Mazama rufina rufina*). It is about 50 cm tall and of a rusty brown colour with a blackish face. Its horns are limited to tiny 8 cm long prongs. One of the smallest and rarest deer in the world is the dwarf Andean pudu (*Pudu mephisto-philes*) which averages under 35 cm in height. It is light greyish-brown and lives in high scrub over 3000 m, usually in the Eastern Cordillera.

Both felines and canines are represented in the *páramo*. The American lion or puma (*Felis concolor*) has been observed around 4000 m and the erroneously named Andean wolf (*Dusicyon cul-paeus*), which is in fact a fox, is also occasionally seen.

The largest Ecuadorian land mammals are the tapirs. The mountain or woolly tapir (*Tapirus pinchaque*) is one of the rarest South American animals, and inhabits the high cloud forests and *páramo* of the Eastern Cordillera from 1500 to 4000 m. It is comparatively common in the Papallacta and Sangay regions, but is extremely difficult to sight because it spends most of its time in thick cover. Its heavy brown body, relatively short legs, large ears and emphatic-ally elongated nose make it unmistakable – if you ever see it! You're more likely to find its tracks, four toes in front and three on the rear foot.

Finally, the smallest bear in the world may be seen in the *páramo* by the extremely lucky and very patient observer. *Tremarctos ornatus*, the Andean spectacled bear, is extremely versatile and has been observed from just above Peru's desert coast to *páramo* at over 4000 m. It is called 'spectacled' because of its irregular light coloured eye patches on its otherwise almost black hair. In Ecuador it has been sighted on both the outside slopes of the Western and Eastern Cordilleras and, as with the woolly tapir, the Papallacta region is favoured.

MINIMUM IMPACT

One look at the areas around base camps and huts on some of the more popular Ecuadorian volcanoes will show you that not all mountaineers are environmentally aware.

Minimum impact means that a place is unchanged by your visit: no garbage, no fire-scars or other damage, no Indians taught to beg by thoughtless handouts of sweets or money.

Don't litter. All your trash should be burned, carried out with you, or disposed of properly at mountain refuges. If you can bring yourself to clean up after less considerate climbers, so much the better.

When nature calls, go well away from the trail, campsite or river, and dig a hole. Bring a light-weight trowel or use your ice axe for the purpose; burn toilet paper.

Don't build fires in the highlands where wood is scarce and is sometimes the only fuel for inhabitants of remote areas. Bring your stove for cooking.

Ecuador's Indians are proud people with their own culture and beliefs. Gratuitous present-giving tends to impose your culture on theirs, so only give gifts or money in return for their help or work. Indiscriminate photography will often alienate you from mountain dwellers. These people, although living under extremely simple conditions, are as sensitive and intelligent as anyone else and resent being treated with arrogance by foreign visitors.

Conservation in Ecuador is the responsibility of the Departamento de Áreas Naturales y Vida Silvestre, under the Ministry of Agriculture. An organisation which helps to protect the flora and fauna of the country is the Fundación Natura. They publish a bimonthly newsletter. The annual subscription is about $US5.

CHAPTER 4
THE CENTRAL VALLEY

INTRODUCTION

Lying in the middle of Ecuador, the Avenue of the Volcanoes is not only the geographical heart of the country but also contains most of its major cities and almost half of the 9 million inhabitants.

The most important city of the Central Valley is of course Ecuador's capital, Quito. Its high mountainous setting is marvellously invigorating and with its well-preserved old town full of narrow cobbled streets and red-tiled colonial buildings, it is the most attractive capital in Latin America. Quito is proud of its eighty-six churches, which, with their intricate wood carvings, superb colonial paintings, and lavish use of gold leaf, are amongst the most splendid in the continent. The church of La Compañía and the monastery of San Francisco, both in the old town, are perhaps the most extravagantly gorgeous. There are some fine museums. The Casa de Cultura at Av. Patria and Av. 12 de Octubre has museums of natural history, modern and 19th century art, musical instruments, and a gallery of changing shows. The Museo del Banco Central on Av. 10 de Agosto has museums of gold, archaeology, and colonial art on the 5th and 6th floors. Information on tourist sights and a map of the city are available from the tourist office on the corner of Avenidas Reina Victoria and Roca in the new town.

You'll probably find yourself staying in Quito for some time as it is not only a charming city but is also well located as a departure point for other areas. Despite being only 25 km from the equator, its altitude (about 2850 m) gives Quito a pleasant climate. This is an excellent elevation to begin acclimatizing for high altitude and the following six easy day hikes near Quito are described with this in mind. These are followed by longer and more difficult hikes and climbs.

SHORT WALKS IN THE QUITO AREA

CERRO PANECILLO (3016 m)

This small hill rises about 160 m above the elevation of Quito and, with the huge statue of the Virgin of Quito at its summit, is a major city landmark.

To climb it go down Calle García Moreno in the old town to where it terminates at Avenida Ambato. From here García Moreno continues as a series of steps and footpaths to the summit – about half an hour of puffing. You can take a No. 22 bus to the top if you don't feel like the exercise. The view is very worthwhile especially early in the morning or in the evening when several volcanoes are often visible.

Looking a few degrees east of south one sees the perfect cone of the famous Cotopaxi with the large black rock known as Yanasacha visible below the summit. Directly below are the jagged peaks of Pasochoa and just to the right is Rumiñahui. To the left of Cotopaxi is Sincholagua, a lumpy mountain sometimes covered with a sprinkling of snow. Looking further left, a little east of southeast one sees the snowcapped bulk of Antisana, the 4th highest mountain in Ecuador. Roughly east is the jagged sawtooth crest of Las Puntas; then at east northeast you'll see the snow dome of Cayambe, Ecuador's 3rd highest mountain, and further left is a long ridge behind which Imbabura and Fuya Fuya appear. Somewhat to the east of north we see Cotacachi, a rather jagged peak occasionally covered with a sprinkling of snow. Due west of Quito is Pichincha, the capital's backyard volcano, and to the southwest is the long ridge of the extinct crater of Atacazo. Finally, rather west of south, is the lump of Iliniza Norte, with the snow peak of Iliniza Sur just visible behind and to the left of it.

If you're feeling extravagant you can eat a meal in the Panecillo restaurant which is one of Quito's finest.

LOMA ILUMBISÍ (3045 m)

This is a long flat hill lying just east of the capital. It is easy to get to and makes a pleasant walk.

Take the No. 8 bus to La Tola (the end of the line) and walk down the hill to the major clover leaf intersection on the southeast side of Quito known as the Los Chillos Autopista (freeway). From here take a bus marked Las Monjas to where there are toll booths on the freeway (or walk southeast along the freeway for about 3 km). From the toll booths head east up the hill. There is a dirt road which switchbacks up the hill but I took short cuts on paths crossing fields. The dirt road reaches the top of the hill and runs north northeast along the summit ridge for over a kilometre before dropping down. Allow about an hour from the toll booth to the highest point.

The easiest way back is the way you came, but it is more interesting to follow the dirt road as it becomes a track through corn fields and eucalyptus groves and then go down the far end of the ridge. After about 45 minutes you'll come to a major fork where you go left. Going right takes you to the village of Cumbaya about 3 km to the east from where there are buses to Quito. Going left soon leads you to the old Quito-Cumbaya road and about 40 minutes walk along this road is a famous Quito church, the Guápulo. You'll pass two bridges in quick succession (over the Río Machángara and the Quebrada El Batán) before reaching the Guápulo and from here it is about a 30 minute walk uphill to the Hotel Quito, or you can take a No. 21 bus into the city.

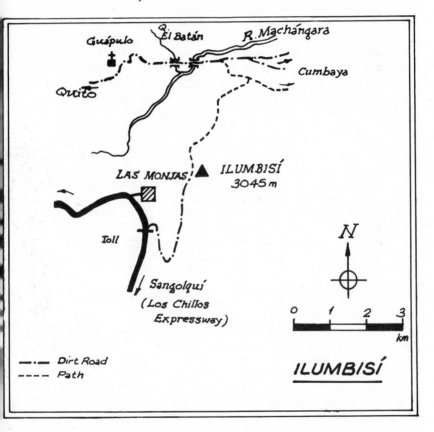

Public telephones are rare in Ecuador. Many small stores will let you make a local call for a few sucres. For long distance calls, go to the telecommunications building, IETEL. There's one in every town.

UNGÜI (3578 m)

This small rounded hill can clearly be seen in a west southwest direction from the Panecillo. The beginning of the walk takes you through Marcopamba which is one of Quito's outlying suburbs and has a rural rather than an urban feel to it. You may even see a couple of llamas wandering by with loads of straw or firewood on their backs. The walk ends with some particularly fine views of the capital.

Start by taking a No. 8 Tola-Pintado bus to its western terminal at Cuartel Mariscal Sucre. Just before the end of the line there is a road at your right called Chilibulo. Follow Chilibulo to the end where it makes a left turn to the southwest, and continue along its zig-zagging route out of town. At any intersection take the major cobbled fork and follow the road through the countryside for about 1½ hours of steady walking which brings you to a pass with a statue of the Virgin Mary. The road down from the pass will eventually bring you to Lloa which is a possible starting point for climbing Pichincha. To climb Ungüi, however, you turn right at the pass. A dirt road heads right and goes around the back of the hill, and in the crotch between this and the road you came up on there is a wide grassy lane which follows an aqueduct (marked *acequia* on the IGM map). This runs underground at the beginning but soon comes to the surface. Follow the aqueduct until you reach the point where there is a full view of Quito. Here you'll find rough tracks heading up and down the hill. At the top of the hill is a tiny stone building. Paths which appear to lead to the top before there is a full view of Quito are just water run offs. If you continue following the aqueduct it will, after some 5 km, join with a rough dirt road heading right and back down the hill towards Marcopamba, or you can make shortcuts downhill through fields if you wish. Half a day is perfectly adequate but if you bring a picnic lunch you'll probably enjoy a full day gazing down on Quito.

This route is shown on the IGM 1:50,000 topographical map of Quito.

PULULAGUA CRATER

The extinct crater of Pululagua is located about 20 km north of Quito and is said to be the largest crater in South America. It is about 4 km wide and 300 m deep; its flat and fertile bottom is used for agriculture and in its centre there is a small hill, Loma Pondoña (2975 m). The floor of the crater is at 2500 m elevation.

To get there take any No. 22 Mitad del Mundo bus which runs from the Panecillo, through the old town, and north on Av. America. About an hour's ride will bring you to Mitad del Mundo where a huge monument marks the equator – though it should be mentioned that the correct equatorial line as determined by the most recent surveys lies several hundred metres away. Get off the bus at the monument and take the good tarmac road to Calacalí to the right of the monument. Walk or get a ride (expect to pay a few sucres) to the turn off for Pululagua which is the first tarmac road to the right, some 4 km beyond the monument. There is no sign at present. Less than a kilometre later this road stops at the very edge of the crater.

From here you can walk down a very steep and winding footpath which is the only access to the crater floor, then walk around on several field roads, or climb the Loma Pondoña in the centre. The descent into and ascent out of the crater take only an hour or so.

NONO HIKES

Nono is a sleepy little village located about 15 km as the crow flies northwest of Quito, but vehicles travelling on the beautiful winding mountain road from Quito to Nono cover twice that distance. The village is interestingly situated on the western flanks of the Western Cordillera and from Nono the road continues to the coast, dropping through lush tropical forests as it does so. This road and the surrounding forest are particularly interesting for the number and variety of bird species. Nono itself is the centre of a fine network of jeep

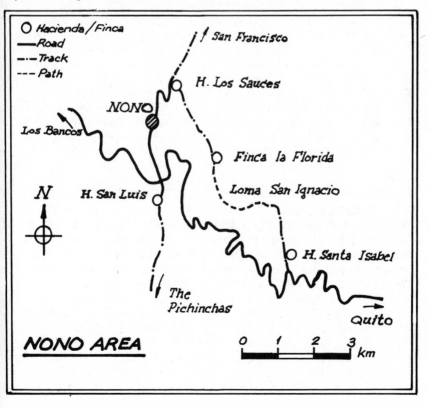

tracks and foot trails going into the surrounding hills, all giving good
day hikes or longer trips if desired. One day hike will be described,
but armed with the IGM 1:50,000 topographical map (predictably
named Nono) you will be able to find plenty of other possibilities.
   You can reach Nono in a couple of hours from Quito. First take the
No. 7 Marin-Cotocollao bus northbound on Av. 10 de Agosto. Get
off at the end of the line which is the Cotocollao plaza. Wait at the
corner of the plaza by the taxi stand for a ride to Nono. There are
occasional buses, and often trucks will stop at this corner and pick
up passengers for Nono and beyond. This ride is very interesting
because after you leave Quito you go past several kilometres of
brickworks. But not brickworks in the sense of the smoke-belching
stacks of Britain's industrial midlands; here you can see *campesinos*
mixing, pouring, forming, drying, firing, and stacking the mud bricks
which are so commonly used in the construction of houses in
Andean villages. The mountain road continues climbing through
pine and eucalyptus plantations until it reaches a pass at nearly
3400 m before dropping down through farmland to Nono at 2700 m.
   From Nono there is a jeep track heading south to Hacienda
San Luis and a footpath continuing south to Loma Yanayacu. You
could continue south walking cross-country to Pichincha. There are
trails east and west of this footpath; I understand that one of the
eastbound trails goes to Quito although I haven't tried it. Trails also
lead to the northwest of Nono to Cerro Chiquilpe and to the north
to San Francisco and beyond. Finally a mixture of tracks and trails
climb southeast out of Nono over Loma San Ignacio and to the pass
on the Quito-Nono road. This is the hike I describe below.
   From where the bus or truck drops you off outside Nono walk
northwest for about a kilometre into the village, then up the main
road until you come to the church plaza at the north end of town.
Turn east on a road which twists and hairpins for over a kilometre to
the Hacienda Los Sauces, and here take the right hand track (which
is still wide enough for a jeep), skirting the *hacienda* and climbing
steadily southeastwards for 2 or 3 km to the Finca La Florida (which
is wrongly marked on the IGM map). After the finca the track
changes into a narrow grassy footpath climbing south and southeast
almost to the top of the hill known as Loma San Ignacio. Go through
two gates and near the top turn right through a third gate. The trail
now widens out again and soon becomes a jeep track which continues for 3 or 4 km past the Hacienda Santa Isabel and onto the
main Quito-Nono road.
   The whole hike will take about 3 hours of steady walking and is
mostly uphill. It could be done in reverse which would be easier. The
beginning of the jeep track is marked by a sign for Hacienda Santa

Isabel on the right hand side of the Quito–Nono road. The uphill route, however, climbs steadily but gently and is good exercise and acclimatization for those planning more strenuous trips into the mountains.

CERRO ILALÓ (3185 m)

Ilaló is a long extinct and heavily eroded volcano near Tumbaco, a small village located 10 km east of and 400 m lower than Quito. The 1:50,000 IGM Sangolquí map clearly shows both mountain

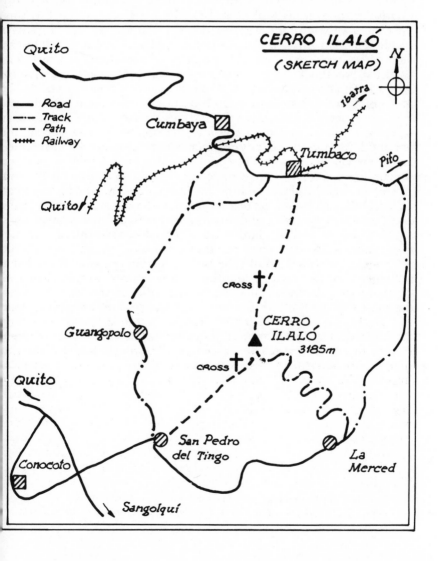

and village. Tumbaco is a delightful place and although essentially Ecuadorian in character it is home to many expatriates working in Quito. Its climate is rather like a warm summer's day in England and its gardens are full of bright tropical flowers, flashing humming-birds, and lazy butterflies.

To get there take a No. 3 bus to the El Batán roundabout from where frequent buses leave for Tumbaco, passing through the village of Cumbaya on the way. Just past the traffic lights on the main road into Tumbaco the bus makes a left hand turn into the town. Get off the bus here and continue walking along the main road for a couple of hundred metres until the first right turn, marked by a sign Jardín Infantil Pestalozzi (as well as an INERHEL sign). Walk up this road for over a kilometre until the road forks. Here take a right fork over a cobbled road marked Centro Comunal Tumbaco. A few hundred metres further you come to a major junction where you turn left. Continue up this road as it passes the last houses and deteriorates into a footpath which you follow until a short distance from the top of a hill. Here you make a sharp left turn off the main trail about a hundred metres beyond a small mud brick house next to a lone pine tree. This trail soon deteriorates into a grassy track zigzagging up the hill and a few minutes later you reach a huge white stone cross which has been visible on and off from the beginning of the walk. You should allow almost 2 hours to reach this cross from the main road.

This is a good place to stop and admire the view but you need another hour of hiking to reach the true summit. Continue past the cross on a narrow but well defined trail which leads up a ridge, along a minor saddle, and up another ridge to a white triangulation marker at the summit. Occasionally the trail forks in which case you should always take the upper trail. The trail fades into grass at times but is generally easy to follow. From the top there is an interesting view of Quito to the northwest, nestling in the valley below Pichincha. To the southwest another white stone cross can be seen; a trail leads past this and down to San Pedro del Tingo. To the southeast there is a dirt road which zigzags its way down to La Merced. Either of these can be used as alternative descent routes. Both places have hot springs and are rather crowded at weekends.

The best Quito newspaper is 'El Comercio'. Apart from local and world news, it will tell you what's on at the cinemas, theatres, and art galleries in town.

LONGER CLIMBS IN THE CENTRAL VALLEY

CERRO IMBABURA (4609 m)

This long extinct volcano is located about 60 km northeast of Quito near the town of Otavalo and the pretty lake of San Pablo. It can be climbed in one long day and although technically an easy climb the extremely rotten rock at the top can make the last metres treacherous. It's first ascent is uncertain; it used to be climbed by local Indians who collected ice and delivered it to the town of Ibarra. There are no longer glaciers on Imbabura and so this industry is now discontinued.

There are no trails and so one has to climb cross-country. Two routes are usually followed. One begins from the village of San Pablo del Lago (accessible by frequent buses from Otavalo) and leaves town from the main square on the road to the right of the church. After about 2 km the road turns right (east) and you continue up a track to the north with the mountain some 5 km directly ahead of you. Head for the highest point and find a gully to take you up to the crater at the top. The rock here is extremely loose and rotten. The highest point is to your left at the western edge of the crater.

The alternative route is from the village of La Esperanza which lies about 9 km northeast of the mountain. The route here is described by Koerner as following the west or right hand side of a dry river bed and up a ridge to the summit. A ridge heading northeast from the summit is shown on the IGM 1:50,000 topographical map (San Pablo del Lago), although I haven't tried it.

La Esperanza is easy to get to: buses leave frequently from Ibarra (20 km north of Otavalo on the Pan American Highway). There are two very cheap and basic hostels in the rather strung out village.

On the outskirts of San Pablo del Lago is the excellent and friendly Hosteria Cusín located in a charming old *hacienda* and run by an Ecuadorian–Australian couple, the Crichtons. Although not for the budget traveller, it is nonetheless extremely good value for money. Horses can be hired for rides in the mountains and the owners are knowledgeable about the area.

CERRO PASOCHOA (4200 m)

This mountain is an ancient and heavily eroded volcano which has been inactive since the last ice age. It is located 30 km south of Quito and is easily identified from the Pan American Highway by its huge half blown away crater open to the west. It is an easy ascent and has been climbed many times from all directions except the west face where the crater walls are extremely steep and rotten. I took a bus to Machachi (frequent buses leave from Quito's Terminal Terrestre) and from the town square followed the east northeast road heading towards Güitig (pronounced wee-tig) where the famous Ecuadorian mineral water comes from. After two hairpin bends and a bridge you reach Güitig some 3 km from Machachi. Turn left at the main store, then right, and almost immediately take another left (just before the church). If in doubt ask for Güitig Alto. Continue on a cobbled road until just beyond Hacienda Mamijudy where you turn left. At the next major fork head right and keep going uphill until you come to a left turn for Hacienda San Miguel. Go through the cobbled and gated paddocks and continue on a dirt road down to a stream. Just before the stream there is a fork; take the left track which leads to a footbridge. Cross the stream and zigzag up the hill, then traverse northeast and head for a saddle south of the mountain. From here head north passing two smaller peaks to your left before reaching the main summit.

You can descend the same way or continue due north, passing an electric plant after some 4 km and joining a dirt road which takes you another 8 km to the main Tambillo–Sangolquí road from where transportation to Quito can be found. This route is often used by local climbers but it is rather difficult to find the correct track off the main road to get you to the mountain. If you do try this way ask for Cuendina; this is where you turn south off the main road.

Pasochoa is on the IGM 1:50,000 Píntag topographical map but if you start from Machachi you'll need the Machachi and Amaguana maps too. You could manage without any maps in clear weather. The round trip can be done in one long day.

THE INCA ROAD TO INGAPIRCA

"I am America!
Genuine, indian, eternal,
The rebellious American stone"
From Ingapirca, Rumishungo by Alejandro Velasco Mejía

INTRODUCTION   At the height of its power the Inca Empire extended from northern Ecuador to central Chile. This huge area was linked by a complex system of well made and maintained roads, the longest of which stretched over 5000 km from Quito to Talca, south of Santiago in Chile. This was the greatest communication system the world had known till that time; greater than the roads of the Roman Empire. Although today the road is in a state of disrepair and in many areas the route has been lost or forgotten it is still possible to find and walk along some remnants of this marvellous road system. One such trail can be found in the southern part of Ecuador's Central Valley and leads to Ingapirca, the most important Inca ruin in Ecuador. This 2 to 3 day hike gives a fascinating glimpse of an Andean rural life which has changed little in hundreds of years.

MAPS   Three 1:50,000 topographical maps cover the route very well. They are the Alausí, Juncal, and Cañar sheets. When I did the hike the latter two were temporarily out of print, so I bought the 1:100,000 Cañar topographical map which covered the area of both unavailable 1:50,000 maps and was almost as good.

GETTING THERE   The nearest town to the beginning of the hike is Alausí where there are several cheap hotels. It is situated just off the Pan American Highway 290 km south of the capital. Buses go there from Terminal Terrestre in Quito, but it may be easier first to go to Riobamba and then change to an Alausí bus at Riobamba's Terminal Terrestre. From Alausí there are occasional buses and trucks in the mornings going to Guasuntos, a small town about 10 km further south on the Pan American Highway, or you could hitch-hike. From Guasuntos ask for the trail to La Moya which lies about a ½ km away and 200 m lower; the trail leaves from the far end of town and heads to the right, avoiding the numerous hairpin bends that make the road much longer. When you reach La Moya stand by the left fork of the road junction to hitch a ride up a steep and spectacular mountain road to the village of Achupallas some 12 km away. There are several trucks a day. You should be able to get from Alausí to Achupallas in a few hours and start walking about midday.

HIKING DIRECTIONS   In Achupallas head for the arch with a cross at

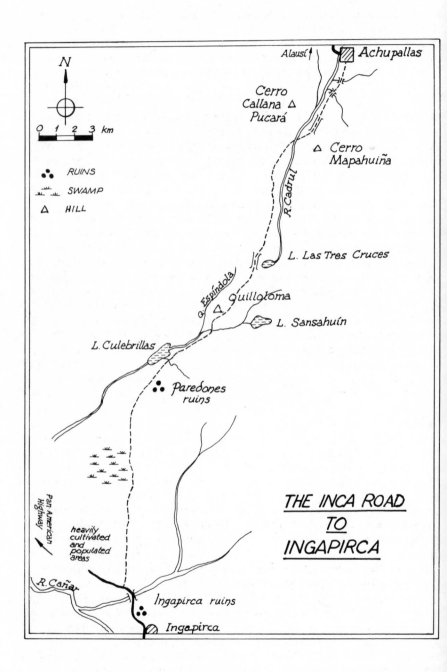

the highest part of the village; take the track left (to the south) of the arch and soon pass the cemetery to your right. The track quickly deteriorates into a stony footpath and crosses a footbridge. At trail junctions continue on the most used trail (usually stony). Some 30 to 40 minutes out of town you recross the river on another footbridge and then follow the left bank of the Río Cadrul (marked the Q. Gadrui on some maps). You are headed for a pass between a pyramidal hill to your left (Cerro Mapahuiña, 4365 m) and a flat-topped hill to your right (Cerro Callana Pucará).

As you get closer to this pass you will see a well-defined notch which you will have to climb. This is interesting as the trail goes up through a hole in the rock: a very tight squeeze. Soon after the notch you should cross the river (it can be jumped) to meet with the trail on the other side. Within a few hundred metres this starts climbing diagonally up the mountain and you reach a height of about 4000 m before the trail contours along the west side of the Río Cadrul valley for several kilometres, reaching the Laguna Las Tres Cruces (by now you are on the Juncal 1:50,000 map). To this lake is about 6 hours of steady hiking from Achupallas but you can find flat spots on the trail to camp on earlier if you wish.

The following day you follow the trail up beyond the lake and across a pass. Beyond the pass the trail becomes rather indistinct; you'll find it crossing some worn rocks and then it rises up to the top of the left hand ridge. Below you is the valley of the Quebrada Espíndola. Walk along the top of this ridge (marked as the Fila de Huagrarumi on the IGM map) and admire the wonderful views as you follow it to its final peak, Quilloloma. To your left is wild trackless countryside with many lakes, the largest of which is Laguna Sansa-huín. This area would doubtless provide several days of excellent off the beaten track camping.

The trail becomes quite distinct again at the top of the ridge and then descends as a rocky path to the left of Quilloloma to the lush and boggy valley bottom beyond. You can quite clearly make out the remains of the old Inca road as a straight line in the grass at the bottom of the valley. At the point where the road crosses the stream you'll find the remains of the foundations of an Inca bridge. This stream has to be crossed; the best place is a little upstream from the bridge where you'll find it narrow enough to jump. There is an obvious trail on the left hand side of the Q. Espíndola which leads you past the southeastern shores of Laguna Culebrillas and to some Inca ruins known as Paredones (ruined walls).

Although it is only an easy half day from Laguna Las Tres Cruces to Paredones this is an excellent place to camp, relax, and enjoy the countryside. The ruin consists of a large main structure whose walls are still more or less standing; there are three main rooms and two smaller ones. The stonework is crude compared to Ingapirca and the famous Peruvian ruins and there is no evidence of typical Inca features such as trapezoidal niches. Around this main structure are the tumbled remains of several smaller buildings. Wildlife is rather limited; I saw caracara hawks and cinclodes. Flowers are prolific however, and you can expect to see gentians, lupins, and daisies among others.

The following day brings you to the ruins of Ingapirca. The walk will take you some 3 to 4 hours and thus leaves you with enough time to explore the ruins and then reach a town to spend the night.

From the Paredones head southwest on the Inca road which is here at its full width of about 7 m. The trail soon swings south and continues straight across the countryside but is extremely boggy. The scenery is rather eerie with huge boulders strewn around like a giant's playthings. Frogs whistle repetitively and brooks bubble up from underground. After 2 or 3 hours the Inca road becomes difficult to follow. There is no specific trail, just walk in a generally south direction and eventually you should be able to see the ruins of Ingapirca in the distance (also south). The terrain shows increasing signs of cultivation and habitation. You end up walking past fields and houses to a road which leads to the ruins themselves.

INGAPIRCA This area was occupied by the Cañaris for some 500 years before the construction of the Inca site. In the 1490s the Inca Huayna Capac conquered the area now known as Ecuador and soon after the construction of Ingapirca (in Quechua, Inca walls) began. It has long been known by academicians, and the plan drawn by La Condamine in 1739 was accurate enough to be used as a basis for the modern excavations of the ruins which began in the late 1960s.

Ingapirca, with its close fitting, mortarless stonework and typical trapezoidal windows and niches, is the finest example of imperial Inca construction in the country, and evidently built by stone masons trained in Cuzco. The precise functions of the site can only be guessed at, but archaeologists think that the most evident and well preserved structure, an elliptical building known as the temple of the sun, had religious or ceremonial purposes. The less well preserved buildings were probably granaries or store houses and part of the complex was used as a tambo, or stopping place for the runners taking messages along the Inca road from Quito to Tomebamba (present day Cuenca).

Ingapirca is 3160 m above sea level. There is a small visitors' hut and a caretaker. A resident archaeologist, Dr Antonio Fresco González, is often available to answer serious questions, and an on site information centre is planned. The nearby village of Ingapirca has a few very basic stores but no accommodation. Trucks leave frequently for the Pan American Highway during the day.

CHAPTER 5
THE WESTERN CORDILLERA

INTRODUCTION
The Central Valley described in Chapter 4 is flanked by the Western and the Eastern Cordilleras. (These are often called the Cordillera Occidental and the Cordillera Real.) The western is lower and less massive, although it does contain Ecuador's highest mountain, the extinct volcano Chimborazo, 6310 m. This mountain range is about 360 km long and 30 to 40 km wide and its average height is 3000 to 3500 m above sea level. All the major mountains and some hikes within the Cordillera will be described systematically, beginning with the northernmost mountain.

VOLCÁN CHILES AND THE PÁRAMO DE EL ÁNGEL
Despite its plural name, Volcán Chiles (4768 m) is a single mountain located on the Colombian border some 24 km west of Tulcán and 130 km northeast of Quito. Although it is extinct, steam vents and sulphur deposits are still found on its slopes and studies of lava flows indicate relatively recent activity. There is a crater which is about 2 km wide and open to the Colombian side. It is an easily and frequently climbed mountain and the ascent can be done in a day. The weather tends to be cloudy and wet with occasional snow so dress accordingly.

There are no topographical maps presently available although the P25 Tufiño 1:50,000 planametric map shows the position of the volcano.

Buses take 5 to 6 hours to reach Tulcán from Quito's northern bus terminals, and there is plenty of accommodation in the town. From Tulcán you must get one of the occasional buses and trucks to Tufiño, some 15 km to the west then head west on the road to Maldonado. You may want to hire a pickup truck to take you about 15 km along this road since there is little traffic. You'll see the mountain to the north (to your right) and the Tufiño–Maldonado road passes within 3 km of the peak. There is no trail so just get off your vehicle at a suitable point and head towards the western ridge of the mountain. You climb up this ridge negotiating small rocky cliffs and a lava 'flow to the main crater from where the summit is easily reached. No rope is required.

The mountain is located in the northern part of the Páramo de El Ángel which is interesting because it is the only area in Ecuador where the giant *frailejon* plant is common. (See *Natural History* in Chapter 3). A walk on the *páramo* here will soon enable you to see these strange plants. One possible walk (which I haven't done) would be some 20 km due south of Volcán Chiles which would take you over the *páramo* to El Ángel, a village on a main road.

CERRO COTACACHI AND LAGUNA DE CUICOCHA

Cerro Cotacachi (4939 m) and Laguna de Cuicocha are located 65 km and 58 km respectively north northeast of Quito. A road leads to the crater called Laguna de Cuicocha which averages 3 km in diameter and is very deep. To get there take any bus from Quito's northern terminals to Otavalo from where frequent buses go to the village of Cotacachi, famous for its leather work. From here a road leads west about 12 km through the village of Quiroga to the lake. Buses occasionally pass by the lake on their way to Plaza Gutiérrez but hiring a pickup truck or hitch-hiking would be faster.

Once at the lake you'll find a rather ritzy hotel and restaurant, with amenities such as boat rides around the islands. Cerro Cotacachi is only about 5 km due north of the northern shore but the weather is often misty thus obscuring visibility.

To climb Cotacachi continue past the lake on the road for a couple of kilometres until you pass a house surrounded by pine trees on the right hand side. Just beyond the house turn right on a cattle trail crossing a field. This trail continues towards the mountain. Unfortunately when I was there two days of incessant rain and 20 m visibility turned my fact finding expedition into a sodden fiasco – I didn't see the mountain at all. Koerner reports that the trail reaches the snow and takes a day. At present there is little or no snow on Cotacachi so I can only assume that the trail does eventually go high up the peak. You then climb up one of two gullies on the west side of the mountain. The rocky and more southerly peak is the highest and the rock is very rotten. Whymper and the Carrels climbed it in 1880, so maybe you will too. Good Luck!

THE PICHINCHAS

INTRODUCTION   The Pichinchas are two volcanoes known as Guagua and Rucu located some 10 km due west of Quito and so easily visible from the capital. They are normally snow free but an occasional high altitude storm will cover them with a brilliant white layer – a pretty sight from the capital.

The two volcanoes are very distinct. Guagua Pichincha, which means baby Pichincha, is the highest and is presently active. Rucu (old) Pichincha is lower, closer to Quito, and inactive. I have read half a dozen different versions of their elevations; the most recent IGM measurements put Guagua at 4794 m and Rucu at an unspecified but slightly lower elevation.

Because of their close position to Quito and Guagua's activity, the Pichinchas have played a great part in both the factual and fictional history of Ecuador's mountains. They are mentioned by the first *conquistadores* and activity is recorded as far back as 1533. The greatest eruption was in 1660 when ash fell up to 500 km from Quito and the capital itself was covered with 40 cm of ash and pumice. The sky was filled with incandescent clouds and the sun was blotted out for 4 days – it must have been a terrifying time for the inhabitants of Quito and the surrounding highlands. Two centuries of inactivity followed. Minor eruptions occurred in 1868, 1869, and 1881. Recent activity in 1981 caused Ecuadorian President Osvaldo Hurtado to fly over the area in a military helicopter for an inspection. Volcanologists claim that the volcano continues to be potentially dangerous although Quito is unlikely to be affected by anything more serious than an ash fall; the topography of the area would cause lava flows and lahars (avalanches of heated snow, earth, and mud) to be diverted to the relatively uninhabited areas to the north, west and south of the volcano.

The climbing history of the volcano goes back further than other Ecuadorian mountains, with 1582 seeing the first recorded ascent by a group of locals led by José Ortiguera. All the famous scientific expeditions of the seventeenth and eighteenth centuries made successful ascents; first La Condamine and Bouguer of the French Geodesic Expedition in 1742, then Humboldt in 1802, and Ecuadorian President Gabriel García Moreno in 1844. The American photographer C. Fardad spent a week taking photographs in the crater in 1867, Reiss and Stübel (the conquerors of Cotopaxi) spent several days there in 1870, and of course Whymper and the Carrels made an almost obligatory ascent in 1880. There were several other ascents during this period. Climbing in the twentieth century has been dominated by Sr. Pedro Esparza, who began climbing in 1926 and has made well over a hundred ascents of the mountain, often alone, thus earning for himself the nickname, 'the solitary of Pichincha'.

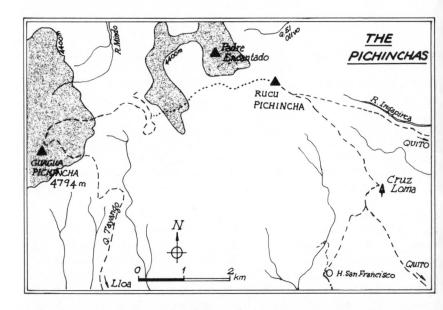

Whymper's second camp on Pichincha.

In 1959 Ecuador's first mountain refuge was built on Pichincha by Fabián Zurita at 4300 m on the northeast side of the mountain. Unfortunately vandals destroyed this soon afterwards and today there are no shelters, but the well-worn footpaths from Quito make this an easy and popular climb.

Various legends have been told about the mountain. One goes back to early colonial days when the inhabitants of Quito didn't dare to climb the volcano because of frequent explosions and eruptions. At last three adventurous Franciscan friars decided to explore but high on the volcano's slopes became lost in a thick fog. Cold and frightened, the three found a cave to shelter in and the bravest went out to investigate the area and look for the way down. A long terrifying storm followed and the friar became hopelessly lost. The storm ended and his two companions left the cave in search of their lost brother, shouting and yelling but with no result. Despondently, they returned to the cave to spend the night. The next morning they went looking for him once again and were overjoyed to see him kneeling in prayer on a high summit. Happily they rushed up to embrace their friend, but their joy turned to terror when they discovered that he'd been turned to stone. They fled back down the mountain and reported to their superiors that the brother had become a rock pillar, praying eternally to God on a peak close to heaven. To this day, Pichincha's third highest peak, lying about halfway in between and a little north of Guagua and Rucu, is named El Padre Encantado (the bewitched priest).

CLIMBING RUCU PICHINCHA

Rucu Pichincha is close enough to Quito that it can be climbed in one long day. An easier hike is a climb up Cruz Loma, the green hill topped by a radio and TV antenna about halfway up Rucu Pichincha, or the hill to the right of Cruz Loma which is known as Loma de las Antenas (Antenna Hill) because it is covered with a veritable forest of TV and radio antennas.

In a modern and expanding city such as Quito the roads and buildings on the outskirts are constantly being changed and improved, hence it is impossible to give absolutely clear cut directions for Rucu Pichincha. Several roads lead from the city into the foothills and any one of the following will eventually lead to paths up the mountains: Av. 24 de Mayo, Av. La Gasca, Calle Alvarez de Cuella (the end of the No. 14 bus route), or Calle Mañosca. This last is my favourite route.

Take one of several buses northbound on Av. América to Calle Mañosca. Walk up this street for about 15 minutes until it crosses the Vía Occidental expressway. Directly opposite Mañosca is a signed road leading to a fertilizer factory; ignore this and take the unsigned road some 50 m to the right (north). Follow this road and take your first left up the hill and then continue taking the uphill fork whenever the road divides. Four wheel drive vehicles and good pick-ups can negotiate this road up to the car park at the top of the 'TV antenna hill' – it is about 15 km and passes a *hacienda* about halfway up. During weekends the hill is used for hang gliding which makes an impressive sight over Quito. A steep hill behind the car park is used by dirt bikers and families come up here to picnic and watch the fun so you shouldn't have any difficulty in hitch-hiking up this hill on sunny weekends.

To reach Rucu Pichincha you take a distinct path which goes to the left of the motorcyclists' hill behind the car park. This path is easily followed for about 2 hours until it meets with another coming up from Cruz Loma. At this point you have two choices; either head right on a path along the bottom of the rocks to a sandy slope which leads to the summit (the easiest way) or head straight up the rocks which are marked with paint splashes or white arrows. This latter route is more direct although perhaps a little hair-raising for beginners. The summit will take a further 1½ hours from the trail junction. There is some rock climbing to be had on Rucu's summit pyramid if you are so inclined – experienced rock climbers will find their own route.

To make the return trip more interesting use another route. If you climbed up the rocks try descending down the sandy slope and follow the trail at the bottom of the rocks to the trail intersection; here take the wide and clear trail back to Cruz Loma. Soon you'll pass a white survey marker and about 1½ hours after leaving the summit you'll reach Cruz Loma. Occasional vehicles will visit it at weekends and you may be able to hitch a ride back to Quito, coming out at the south end of the city after a long and zigzagging ride. If you are walking however, the quickest route is straight down the hill to the city, following a faint path underneath the electric pylons from the TV and radio antenna. This will bring you out in the La Gasca area. There are other paths as well if you feel in an exploratory mood.

If you just want to visit Cruz Loma you must climb from La Gasca or from Av. 24 de Mayo – the latter is the less steep way. There is no easy way to reach Cruz Loma from the Antenna hill except by going to the rocky foot of Rucu Pichincha as described.

CLIMBING GUAGUA PICHINCHA

This is a 2 day trip so come prepared to camp out. Carry water as it is not available higher up. The usual route to Guagua is via Rucu Pichincha. From behind the summit continue on a distinct path marked with paint splashes. This becomes less distinct after a while but Guagua is the only big mountain a little south of west so you can't miss it. The crater is about 1½ km in diameter and 700 m deep with a small 400 m cone in the crater floor. This cone produces the greatest amount of volcanic activity. The best camping spot is near a small sulphurous lake between the cone and the eastern wall of the crater. In the east wall of the cone there is reportedly a yellow sulphur-encrusted cave which is 5 m wide and contains sulphurous stalactites of a metre in length – I've never found it.

An alternative and shorter route to Guagua, avoiding Rucu completely, is via the village of Lloa. Take a No. 8 Tola–Pintado bus along Av. Vencedores de Pichincha (formerly Av. Bahía de Caráquez) to the end of the line at Cuartel Mariscal Sucre. Just before the end of the line take a road to the right up the hill on Av. Chilibulo and follow this as it winds through the suburb of Marcopamba, past pine plantations to a pass 6 km away, which is marked by a statue of the Virgin. From the pass a winding road drops into the valley and after 4 km reaches the agricultural village of Lloa. You can walk this route or take one of the occasional buses from Av. Chilibulo in Quito or hitch-hike. Near the beginning of the village make a right turn, leaving the church to your left. If the weather is dry, a good vehicle can go a considerable way up the mountain on dirt roads; you can also enquire in Lloa about mule hire from one of the nearby *haciendas*. In a vehicle (or on foot) follow the road past the church, past a sign for Granja Ovina, past a right hand fork until you reach a Y junction about 4 km from Lloa. Here you take the right fork. About 4 km further up a flat area is used for parking. From here head uphill to Guagua's summit following a vague trail more or less north. It takes about 4 hours to reach the top and you'll lose the trail and start heading cross-country. The vegetated areas are a little easier than the loose volcanic scree because the *páramo* is high enough here to discourage the growth of thick bushes. There are no technical problems and the round trip can be done in a long day from Lloa.

There is also an approach from the north, although I haven't met anyone who has done it. Head to the village of Nono (see *Nono Hikes* in Chapter 4) and then head south on a jeep track to Hacienda San Luis and continue south on paths and then cross-country to the Pichinchas.

The paths feather-lined and steep.
Overhead a sky of mud.
Then all of a sudden in the air the purest white lily of a tall volcano.
                                                                    Henri Michaux

CERRO ATACAZO (4457 m)

IN THE CRATER OF MOUNT ATACATZHO 14,742 FEET

Crater? ah!
We were expecting something more serious...
Ah!...

It would be nice to come upon something a bit more serious...
Crater? Indeed? Ah!
We're used to insisting upon something a bit serious.
But what is this laughing valley?
What is this laughing doing here?
These dwarf plant Japanese gardens,
This bit of shaved lawn (because of the awfulness of the climate,
of course, but so what?)
This imitation of a flowerbed border? this moss?
And this indoor mildness, this refuge
This picnic site, this springtime
We didn't come here looking for spring
We came to look for a volcano.

Outside, meanwhile, there's a hell of a cold wind blowing – which shows how high up we are. It angrily erupts down out of the one existing window in the circular crest, along with all the chunks of cloud that it has come upon en route, and which it sweeps off whole into the volcano.

From 'Ecuador: A Travel Journal' by Henri Michaux, 1928

Atacazo is an ancient and eroded volcano located about 20 km southwest of Quito. With a four wheel drive vehicle you can drive to within an hour of the summit; if relying on public transport this is a two day trip. It is not a difficult climb and, unusual in Ecuador, the rocky summit is not composed of rotten and dangerous rocks but is quite solid.

Begin by taking a bus to Chillogallo from Plaza 24 de Mayo in Quito's old town, and walking 3 km west on the old Santo Domingo road (it's the only westbound highway) to the village plaza in La Libertad. Alternatively the more expensive and faster microbus will take you from 24 de Mayo all the way to La Libertad. From here you will find occasional trucks (or you can walk or hitch-hike) as far as San Juan, a tiny village about 10 km to the west. A beautiful mountain road climbs and hairpins steeply from La Libertad at 3000 m to San Juan, at about 3450 m. Continuing westward from San Juan the old highway now drops down giving fascinating opportunities to observe the ecological changes from 3450 m to sea level

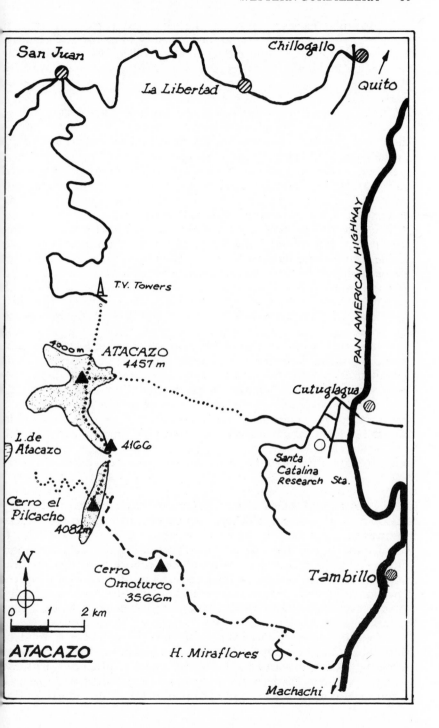

ATACAZO

and providing excellent birding. To climb Atacazo, however, yo
leave San Juan on a southbound jeep road heading towards some T\
and radio antennas. Anyone in the village will point out the road; i
reaches the antennas in 10 to 12 km, but there is almost no traffic
If you need drinking water you'll pass near the last streams abou
2 to 3 km before the end of the road.

From the antennas head south up gently sloping, grassy *páram*
(the "bit of shaved lawn" of Michaux's poem) to an obvious notch i
the crater rim. It is an easy walk which will take a little over an hou
From here the highest point is to your left; a gentle scramble ove
grass and rocks. Below you is the delicately coloured crater, wid
open to the west, and filled with pastel shades of sand and lava an
brighter splashes of vegetation. It is not difficult to scramble dow
and explore "These dwarf plant Japanese gardens".

The descent can be made in different ways. The shortest is to hea
almost due east across the *páramo* for about 7 km until you reac
the Estación Experimental Santa Catalina which lies roughly a kilc
metre west of the Pan American Highway. (This is also a commo
ascent route.) A more interesting descent is to head south on th
crater rim for about a kilometre beyond the highest point, then hea
southeast along an obvious ridge to a small hill (4166 m) about
kilometre away; from here head south southwest along another ridg
to a long flattish hill (Cerro El Pilcacho, 4082 m) almost 2 km away
A short distance before you reach the top of El Pilcacho you'll fin
a trail crossing the ridge. Westward, it winds through interestin
looking *páramo* to Laguna de Atacazo some 3 km away; eastward i
soon joins a trail heading southeast towards Cerro Omoturco, 3566 m
2 km away. From Omoturco a dirt road winds 7 to 8 km to Haciend
Miraflores from which a road continues a further 2 to 3 km to th
Pan American Highway. If you go north along the Highway for abou
3 km to Tambillo, it will be easier to catch buses to Quito.

EL CORAZÓN (4788 m)

Corazón is an ancient, eroded, and extinct volcano about 40 k
southwest of Quito. The first recorded ascent was in 1738 by L
Condamine and Bouguer and this easy peak has been climbed man
times since. Preconquest ruins have been reported on the northeas
slopes, but they are very overgrown and have yet to be investigatec
The name Corazón means 'heart' and is said to refer to two gullie
on the northeast slopes which, when seen from a distance, appea
to join together roughly in the shape of a heart.

To get there take a bus from Quito's Terminal Terrestre to Macł
achi, then walk south on the Pan American Highway for 2 km beyon
the left fork leading into Machachi (by a large Güitig billboard) unt
you see a signed road on the right hand side leading to Aloasí. G
through Aloasí on a good cobbled road as far as the railway statior

3 km from the Pan American Highway. The road then continues as a
dirt track which eventually peters out on the *páramo*. Head more or
less due west across the *páramo* to a saddle on the north side of the
peak and from here turn left (south) to the summit. Allow about 5
hours of steady hiking from the railway station to the summit.

There is another route from the north. About 5 km before Machachi there is a right turn onto a major road leading to Santo Domingo
and the coast. Follow this road about 3 km to Alóag and at the railway station just beyond Alóag take a left fork down an old dirt road.
Between 11 and 12 km down this road you'll find the Hacienda La
Granja where it is possible to hire mules. From here head south
across the *páramo* about 6 km to the peak, reaching the saddle on
the north side as described in the first route.

Note: the Corazón map is on page 73

Machachi and Corazón.

THE ILINIZAS

INTRODUCTION   These are two peaks located about 55 km south southwest of Quito. Iliniza Sur (5263 m) has the distinction of being the sixth highest mountain in the country whilst Iliniza Norte (5126 m) is the eighth highest. Prehistorically they were one volcano but today the two peaks are separated by a saddle and are about 1½ km away from one another. Jean and Louis Carrel of Whymper's expedition logged the first ascent of Iliniza Sur in May 1880, but Whymper himself never reached the summit despite two attempts in February and June of the same year. The first ascent of Iliniza Norte was interesting in that it was one of the few first ascents made by Ecuadorian climbers and the only Ecuadorian 'first' of one of the country's ten peaks of over 5000 m. Ecuador's Nicolás Martínez accompanied by Alejandro Villavicencio reached the summit in March 1912.

There is a simple refuge known as Refugio Nuevos Horizontes at 4650 m just east of and below the saddle linking the two mountains. It can accommodate about two dozen persons but has no facilities and there are recent reports of damage by vandals. Water is obtained from the stream running a few metres away from the hut. The area is covered by the IGM 1:50,000 Machachi topographical map.

ACCESS   About 40 km south of Quito and 5 km south of Machachi on the Pan American Highway there is an unsigned right turn for the small community of El Chaupi. The turn off is at a place known locally as Tarqui about 100 m before a bridge (not after the bridge as indicated on the IGM map). Buses bound for Latacunga pass this turn off, or you can take a bus to Machachi and walk or hitch-hike. From the Pan American Highway to El Chaupi is about 7 km of cobbled road; there are occasional trucks acting as buses and a few private vehicles.

At El Chaupi turn right onto the road behind the church. The surface changes from cobbles to dirt. Walk or drive up this dirt road for about 3 km until you come to a cross on the right hand side. Take the left turn about 200 m beyond this cross. This road goes through fields, then through an avenue of pine trees, past the Hacienda El Refugio, and after 3 km begins twisting and climbing past the Lomo Pilango. About 3 km of climbing brings one to a shrine. This point, approximately 16 km from the Pan American Highway, is a parking area although with a four wheel drive vehicle you can continue up the very badly gullied road for another 2½ km. The road then deteriorates into a footpath leading to a sandy ridge. A trodden path heads up this ridge and a short way from the top veers right to the refuge. You cannot see the refuge until you are almost there. From the final driveable point to the refuge is 1 to 2 hours on foot; from El Chaupi to the refuge takes more than half a day.

CLIMBING ILINIZA NORTE (5126 m)

Despite the glacier marked on IGM maps, Iliniza Norte is a rocky mountain with no permanent snow. It can easily be climbed in 2 hours from the refuge. Technical equipment is unnecessary.

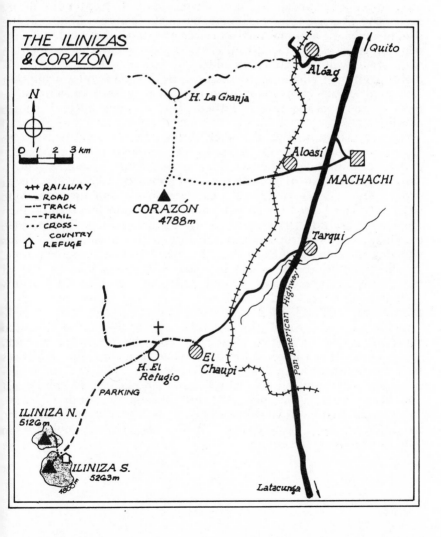

From the refuge walk across the saddle between the two mountains and climb up the southeast ridge of Norte. The ridge narrows about halfway up and crosses the 'Paso de Muerte' (Death Pass) which is far easier to cross than its name implies. The summit is a near vertical wall which is best avoided by skirting it to the right for 200 to 300 m and then climbing left to the top. The climb is easy except for the last few metres which are the usual rotten rock.

CLIMBING ILINIZA SUR (5263 m)

This relatively steep and crevassed mountain is one of the more difficult climbs in the country, and is not for beginners. Some of the steeper sections are about sixty degrees and so front pointing is necessary. This is a tiring technique, particularly at over 5000 m, and should be learnt and practised at lower elevations if possible (in the Alps or the Rockies for example). Protection such as ice screws or snow stakes will be required by all except extremely experienced and highly confident climbers. Rockfall can be a hazard and a helmet is suggested. Avalanches occur often enough to pose a danger and a detailed route description is difficult due to constantly changing conditions.

The normal route is via the north face and begins from the Nuevos Horizontes hut then heads west into the saddle between the north and south mountains. About a ½ km from the hut climb up a gently sloping rock-strewn snow-field and then ascend an increasingly steep snow gully between two large rock outcrops. Several crevasses will have to be negotiated (often you can climb around them) until you reach the east ridge. Here you go right and head for the top, by-passing a rocky outcrop known as 'el hongo' (the mushroom) before reaching the summit of Iliniza Sur. The descent is via the same route. In good conditions the round trip can be done in 6 hours, but a full day is not uncommon. You should plan a pre-dawn departure to minimize rockfall and avalanche danger caused by the melting of the snow in the midday sun.

A more difficult route is known as the east ridge or Celso Zuquillo route (after one of its first climbers). From the hut go left around the mountain for a few hundred metres and then climb up what is in fact the northeast ridge which has heavy rime build up. The most difficult route of all was done by Ecuadorian climbers Joseph Bergé and Marco Cruz in October 1973 and goes up the south ridge. A bivouac and highly technical ice climbing are required and the route has rarely, if ever, been repeated. World class climbers could probably force other routes too.

HIKING AND CLIMBING IN THE
CHIMBORAZO–CARIHUAIRAZO AREA

*"Señor, we understand perfectly, that in an affair like yours, it is
necessary to dissemble – a little; and you, doubtless, do quite
right to say you intend to ascend Chimborazo – a thing that
everyone knows is perfectly impossible. We know very well what
is your object! You wish to discover the TREASURES which are
buried in Chimborazo . . ."*

Edward Whymper, 1892.

INTRODUCTION   Chimborazo is located 150 km south southwest of
Quito. Some 10 km northeast of it lies its sister volcano Carihuairazo. Both are ancient and extinct volcanoes. Carihuairazo's rather
jagged shape indicates a younger mountain whilst the rounded bulk
of Chimborazo testifies to its great age. It is an extremely massive
mountain which volcanologists claim is composed of the remnants of
two volcanoes.

Chimborazo is, at 6310 m, the highest mountain in the country
and for many years was thought to be the highest in the world. It
still retains the distinction of being the point on the earth's surface
which is farthest from its centre; this is due to the earth's equatorial
bulge. It is higher than any mountain in the Americas north of it:
McKinley is about 75 m lower. Chimborazo's reputation as such a
high mountain led to many attempts on the summit during the seventeenth and eighteenth centuries before it was climbed by Whymper
and the Carrels in 1880. Carihuairazo is also an impressively high
peak; at 5020 m it ranks ninth in height in Ecuador and was conquered, also in 1880, by the Whymper expedition with the Ecuadorians David Beltrán and Francisco Campaña.

Both mountains are snow capped and snow and ice climbing
equipment and technique are required for their ascents. The normal
routes are relatively straightforward. For the non-climber, an excellent hike is from the Pan American Highway to the Ambato–Guaranda
road. This crosses the pass between the two mountains with beautiful views of these and other major peaks. For the mountaineer,
combining the hike with ascents of both peaks provides an exceptional experience.

*I live not in myself, but I become
Portion of that around me; and to me
High mountains are a feeling, but the hum
of human cities torture.*

                               Byron

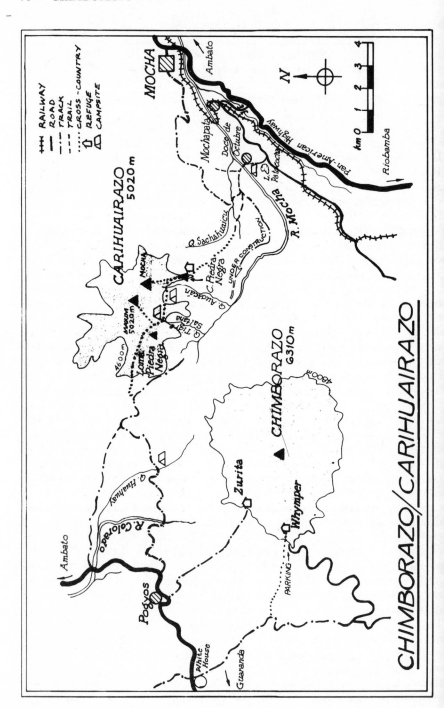

CHIMBORAZO/CARIHUAIRAZO

MAPS   Two 1:50,000 topographical maps from the IGM cover the area: the Quero and Chimborazo sheets. The glaciers on the mountains are inaccurately represented; they have greatly receded in recent years and on Carihuairazo occupy barely half of the area assigned to them on the maps. Thus part of the hike appears to cross glaciers but this is not so. Most of the other topographical features are accurate.

DIRECTIONS FOR HIKERS

From Quito's Terminal Terrestre take a Riobamba bus along the Pan American Highway. About half-way between Ambato and Riobamba you will see a sign on your right for Mocha. Stay on the bus for a further 5 to 6 km as the road climbs steeply until a turn off to Mochapata. There is no sign; the right hand turn off is a steeply descending cobbled road which soon crosses the Quebrada Yanayacu via a stone bridge which is plainly visible from the highway. Allow about 3 hours on the bus from Quito.

Walk down the cobbled road, cross the stone bridge, and look for trails climbing the small hill in front of you. Take one of these over the hill (avoiding a detour through Mochapata), cross a railway track, and you will soon come to a rough road where you turn left. In clear weather Chimborazo's steep and rugged southeastern flanks are visible to the west; this side provides the most difficult ascent routes and the view is splendid. Carihuairazo is seen to the northwest but from this angle the major glaciers are not properly appreciated.

Walk about 3 km along the road until you come to a right hand turn onto a dirt road passing the swampy Laguna Patococha and continuing about a kilometre to the unsigned settlement of Doce de Octubre at about 3560 m and not marked on the IGM map. You may be allowed to sleep in the village hall (four bare walls, no facilities). Alternatively continue about a kilometre along the steeply descending dirt road to the banks of the Río Mocha where you can camp. If you have a heavy load of gear, you can rent mules in Doce de Octubre (though this may take 2 or 3 days to arrange) to take you to the hut at the base of Carihuairazo. A four wheel drive vehicle will reach the settlement after which you must rely on mule or man power.

From the village to the refuge on Carihuairazo (at about 4300 m) takes 5 to 8 hours with a pack. Cross the Río Mocha and follow the deteriorating track up towards a flat area known as Mauca Corral. Turn left off the track and head north and then west around the northwest end of Loma Tulutuz which is the large flat-topped hill in front of you after you have crossed the river. After about a kilometre of cross-country hiking you will run into a footpath around the back of Loma Tulutuz. Follow this for another kilometre until you can see two sharp ridges heading northwest towards Carihuai-

razo. They are separated by a small river, the Quebrada Sachahuaicu
Cross a stream and climb the left hand ridge (Filo de Sachahuaicu
and follow cow paths along the gently rising ridge top which head
west and then curves northwest toward Cerro Piedra Negra (c. 4480 m
which is a southern spur of Carihuairazo and about 4 km away. Keep
your eyes peeled for the small hut about ½ km to the east of Cerro
Piedra Negra and by the right flank of a small conical hill. When you
seem to be heading away from the hut, leave the ridge and go north
cross-country towards it. There are no facilities; it is a dilapidated
wooden structure which could sleep eight people at a squeeze. There
are a few pools of brown water nearby which is all right to drink
after boiling or sterilizing.

The hut is used as a base to climb the Mocha peak of Carihuairazo
(see *Climbing Carihuairazo*). From the hut it is an easy scramble to
the top of Cerro Piedra Negra from which there are views of Ambato
as well as four major peaks: Carihuairazo to the north, Chimborazo
to the southwest, Tungurahua to the east, and El Altar to the south
east. Accurate information on this hut is hard to come by. Several
local climbers told me that it didn't exist and others said that they
had looked for it but couldn't find it. Don't be put off by such
reports – it's there!

From the hut the hiker continues roughly westwards along the
south flanks of Carihuairazo. First climb onto the ridge joining Cerro
Piedra Negra with Carihuairazo and continue north along it for
about a kilometre until you are near the head of the Aucacán river
valley on your left. Then drop down from the ridge, cross the Que
brada Aucacán high up by the central glacier of Carihuairazo, and
scramble up the opposite side of the Aucacán valley to the top of the
ridge. It's easier than it looks, especially if you follow the diagonal
slash of vegetation which is clearly visible on the far side. At the top
are flat camping areas with melt water running off nearby. Other
good campsites are found near lakes at the head of the Quebrada
Tigre Saltana valley, about ½ an hour roughly west from the ridge
Both sites are often used as base camps for the ascent of Carihuai
razo's main (Maxim) peak (see *Climbing Carihuairazo*). Allow a half
day to reach this area from the hut. This is such a pretty area that
it is worth camping early and exploring. A good side trip is to the
western flanks of Carihuairazo where many interesting high Andean
lakes, streams, and bogs can be investigated.

The hike continues roughly north over a pass between Carihuai
razo and Loma Piedra Negra (not to be confused with Cerro Piedra
Negra), a pyramidal peak west of Carihuairazo. There is a trail
around the eastern and northern flanks of Loma Piedra Negra. It is
rather indistinct in places but frequent cairns are an aid. Once you
have rounded Loma Piedra Negra the trail fades and you strike west
down a gently sloping plain for about 3 km until you come to a road
This is quite accurately marked on the IGM map and by comparing

the curves of the road with the map you can soon see where you are. Walk about 6 km along the road until you cross the Quebrada Huahuay. Camp here because this is the last place you'll get water before reaching the Ambato–Guaranda road which is about 8 km. further. (The Río Colorado, halfway between the Q. Huahuay and the Ambato–Guaranda road, is often dry.)

On the final day walk out 8 km to the main road. Here you can flag down a bus to take you into Ambato (turn right) or Guaranda (turn left). For ascents of Chimborazo it is 1 to 2 km to Pogyos (the old standard route) or about 6 km to the turn off for the Whymper refuge (the new normal route) in the direction of Guaranda.

CLIMBING CARIHUAIRAZO
There are two main peaks, Maxim in the centre and Mocha in the southeast. The former is the highest at 5020 m (IGM figures) although some authorities put Maxim at 5116 m and Mocha at 5030 m. Whatever the correct altitude, both peaks are snow covered and require snow and ice climbing experience, though not of a particularly high technical standard.

The hut at 4300 m (described earlier) on the southeastern slopes of the mountain is used by climbers of the Mocha peak. The Maxim peak requires a tented base camp (the best area is the lakes at the head of Quebrada Tigre Saltana) and for a shorter approach than the one described in the hiking directions start from the Ambato–Guaranda road. The dirt road leading to Carihuairazo is unsigned and difficult to find, however. Ask around 1 to 2 km before Pogyos – if you can find someone – for the road to Carihuairazo. Some people know the area at the base of the mountain as Abraspungo.

Maxim Peak is most easily climbed by the Direct Route. From the lakes campsite go right onto a ridge and follow this to the base of the glacier. Climb directly up and then left around a huge rocky outcrop in the centre of the glacier. Then climb straight up avoiding the crevasses, most of which can be easily rounded or stepped over. A large crevasse has opened up about 100 m below the summit but a snow bridge can normally be found. The top few metres are rocky and there is some danger from rockfall. Allow 2 to 3 hours for the ascent.

The Variant of the Direct Route can be climbed by heading straight up the glacier in front of the base camp and passing to one's right the huge rock outcrop mentioned in the Direct Route description. There are more crevasses on this route. The North Cornice Route begins below the rock outcrop and heads left over a ridge towards the left hand horizon, then climbs over a rock band and heads for the summit.

The Mocha Glacier is steeper and quite heavily crevassed and provides an interesting route-finding problem; it can be climbed directly from the Carihuairazo hut in 4 to 6 hours. A pleasant alternative is to place a high camp at the base of the glacier.

From the hut climb up onto the ridge joining Cerro Piedra Negra with Carihuairazo and follow the ridge for about a kilometre. Flat spaces are found at the end of the ridge for a high camp (melt water available). There is no standard route because the steep glacier is constantly changing. I climbed up scree along the left hand side of the lower glacier, then climbed onto the glacier above the serac field at its tongue and skirted the large ice fall in the centre of the glacier (but beware of rock fall from the cliffs bordering the ice). I then picked my way through, around, and over several crevasses until I reached the top of the glacier. The summit is to the right and is composed of rather rotten rock. The glacier is small and not especially difficult, but a lot of fun is had finding your way.

CLIMBING CHIMBORAZO

There are five summits: the Whymper (or Ecuador) summit at 6310 m, the Veintimilla summit at 6267 m, the North summit at about 6200 m, the Central (or Polytechnic) summit around 6000 m, and the Eastern (or Nicolás Martínez) summit of approximately 5500 m. The last, although the lowest, is the most difficult. The routes to the highest summit will be discussed more thoroughly.

There are two normal routes which are known as the old and the new. The Old Route ascends the northwest flanks following Whymper's second ascent route. The New Route, also known as the Whymper Route, follows his first ascent on the southwestern flanks of the mountain. Although the New Route has traditionally been labelled as the more difficult it is now the most popular, especially since the opening of the new Edward Whymper refuge in 1980. Receding glaciers are making the Old Route less straightforward.

THE NEW (WHYMPER) ROUTE   The best way to reach the mountain is by bus from Ambato to Guaranda. Sit on the left hand side of the bus for the best views. About 56 km from Ambato you will come to a dirt road on your left leading to the Whymper refuge. This road is marked by a deserted white house of cement blocks on the left hand side, immediately beyond the junction. It is the only house on the left hand side for many kilometres. From the junction walk southeast on the dirt road for 3 to 4 km until you come to a hairpin bend. Here you can turn left up a small gully and climb due east for a further 3 to 4 km until you see the parking area below the refuge. Allow 3 to 6 hours from the junction to the car park (the high altitude slows you down). If you don't want to go cross-country you can follow the road around to the parking area but this is 10 to 12 km. There is a narrow trail leading from the upper right part of the parking area to the refuge about 200 m above and half an hour away.

It is possible to come from Riobamba but with considerably

more difficulty as there are no nearby buses. One way is to take a taxi via San Juan and then on dirt roads across the *páramo*; over 40 km, and best with an experienced driver or guide as it is easy to lose your way.

The refuge is well appointed with bunk beds for about three dozen mountaineers (use your own sleeping bag), toilets, cold water, a kitchen with utensils and a propane gas stove (though this has been known to run out of gas during and after a busy weekend), a small supply of basic foods for sale, an electric generator, a fireplace, and a huge visitor's book with which to while away high altitude storms. There is a hut guardian who will keep an eye on your belongings when you climb; he will also charge you a fee of less than US $2 per day to use the hut.

To climb the New or Whymper route head right from the refuge up scree slopes to the prominent rock spires known as Whymper's Needle. Follow the obvious ridge up from the needle to a rock band about 30 m high. Several snow/ice gullies offer access through the rock band. One of the central gullies is the easiest; the angle is about fifty degrees and so front pointing will be needed. Above the rock band is a fairly steep snow-field which is best climbed by zigzagging. Towards the top of this snow-field there is another large rock band to your right, but the route traverses under seracs to the left hand horizon. The top of the snow-field and the traverse are usually marked with flags and footprints. There is objective danger from ice fall from the seracs above the traverse. At the end of the traverse the route heads directly up toward the summit, again usually marked by flags and footprints. There are several small crevasses here. You reach the Veintimilla peak from where it is nearly a kilometre east over a gentle snow basin to the main summit. Late in the day this snow basin is filled with notoriously soft snow and at this altitude it takes great energy to wade through thigh deep snow. Therefore it is advisable to start as early as possible (midnight) so that the final slog to the summit is easier. Some climbers have spent the night near Veintimilla summit and finished the climb the next day – this is an adventure for experienced, acclimatized, and well equipped climbers. 8 to 10 hours are normally needed for the ascent (although I know of one party which took 20 hours!). Allow 3 to 4 hours for the descent.

Experienced climbers can reach the top with just ice axe, crampons, and rope. Less experienced climbers may want the security of a second tool (ice hammer) for the steeper sections (the icy gully through the first rock band) and some ice screws, snow stakes, and deadmen for protection.

The major drawback to the Whymper route is the danger from falling seracs above the high traverse. Although not a daily occurrence, this possibility may make you want to consider a more direct route which avoids these dangers. Although shorter, the Direct

Route is steeper and technically more challenging, although still not extremely hard. It climbs directly up the Thielmann Glacier to the left of the hut and meets the Whymper route at the end of the traverse. Route finding up the Thielmann Glacier is a problem and so this is for climbers who have route-finding ability. Flags and footprints are often found but cannot be relied upon.

THE OLD ROUTE The old route begins at the village of Pogyos (also spelt Poggios or Pogyo) which is a tiny group of buildings on a bend of the road about 50 km south of Ambato on the road to Guaranda. About 1 and 4 km before Pogyos are two roads to the left which may help you find it; the bus driver sometimes knows it.

Pogyos is the last place on the route where you can find water, but you'll probably want to sterilize it. Mules can be hired inexpensively to carry water and your gear up to the Fabián Zurita refuge at 4900 m – about 900 m above Pogyos. To get to the refuge cross the Ambato–Guaranda road and follow a dirt track that leaves the road a few hundred metres west of Pogyos and heads southeast across the sandy *páramo* to the hut which is 3 or 4 hours' walk away.

The hut was built in 1964 and is the oldest still in use in Ecuador. The orange octagonal shelter is now in a very dilapidated condition with a door that doesn't close properly, a leaky roof, and plenty of trash scattered around. Nevertheless it provides basic shelter for about ten people.

The climb from the hut to the summit is becoming more demanding as the glacier recedes. The route goes up the loose scree above the hut to the snowline and then continues on the snow to the base of a large, red, rock band known as the 'murallas rojas' (red walls). At the base of the red walls traverse to your right and continue upwards on snow along or a little beyond the right edge of the walls. Once beyond the walls head towards the peak above you, watching for crevasses which will be predominantly to your right. As you get high on the peak start heading left and to the side of it – this peak is the second or Veintimilla peak. The rounded summit is about a kilometre east of Veintimilla. The climb takes from 8 to 12 hours. A midnight departure is recommended as the summit snow plateau becomes very soft and slushy and avalanche danger on the slopes increases after midday.

When I tried this route I found that the glacier had receded so much that the scree slog up from the hut took several hours. A huge bergschrund had formed between the scree and the glacier and it was difficult to find an easy way onto the snow. Although this climb proved a failure, I found the new Whymper route fairly straightforward. With the good new Whymper hut now available I would suggest the new route as being the best – unless you actually like slogging up loose scree at 5000 m!

OTHER ROUTES   Many new routes remain to be climbed on a mountain of this size. There are also routes which have had only one or two ascents. Among these are the following: the eastern summit via the Moreno glacier in the southeast, the main summit from the north, and the central peak via the Humboldt glacier in the south. These routes are suggestions for highly advanced climbers only. Otherwise stay on the standard routes; if you need a guide see the appropriate section in Chapter 3.

Chimborazo can be and is climbed year round but June and July are considered the best months. August tends to be windy and September is not too bad, but October and November have long spells of bad weather. Late December and early January are good, but the rest of the year has predominantly bad weather, with April the worst month. A tent is only needed by hikers doing the full route described.

LAS CAJAS NATIONAL RECREATION AREA

At the southern end of the Western Cordillera is found an enchantingly beautiful area of *páramo*. This region of rolling hills and sparkling lakes is rarely visited – a fact that adds to its charm. For the naturalist the principal attraction is the variety of plants and a careful ornithologist will see a good number of bird species. The hiker is faced with a profusion of lakes of all shapes, sizes, and colours; the area boasts 275 named lakes and countless minor ponds and tarns. This is the Las Cajas National Recreation Area, a reserve of almost 29,000 hectares set aside for preservation in 1977.

The preserve lies about 29 km west of Cuenca. This charming city, the nation's third largest, is worth a few days' exploration. Getting a bus for the 10 hour trip to Cuenca from Quito's Terminal Terrestre is straightforward and once in Cuenca you should visit the tourist information office which is on the Cathedral Square known as Parque Abdón Calderón. Here you can obtain city maps, maps of Las Cajas (they are not available within the park), and brochures about the area. A permit, costing less than a dollar, is required to pass the night in Las Cajas; this is also obtainable from the helpful tourist office, along with up to date information on how to get there.

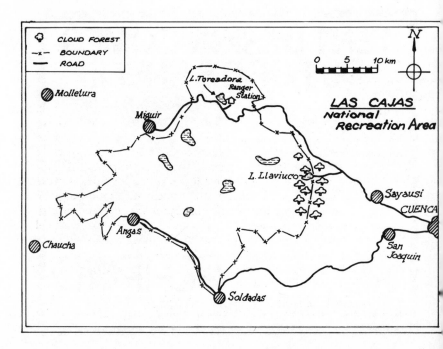

There is at least one bus a day which leaves at 6.30 a.m. from
Plaza San Sebastián at the corners of Bolívar and Coronel G. Talvot.
The bus is marked Sayausi-Miguir and takes about 2 hours to reach
the park information centre and ranger station by Laguna Toreadora
in the northern part of the park. There are a few bunks and a kitchen
here; for a modest fee you can sleep in the station by prior arrangement. Camping is permitted throughout the park and is free. Another
route into the park is on the bus to Angas, on the southwestern
border of Las Cajas. Buses leave from Av. Loja by the river on
Tuesday, Wednesday, Friday, and Saturday at 6.30 a.m.

Once you get away from the immediate environs of the park
station you will find a noticeable lack of trails and signs. Any trails
you do find will usually peter out fairly quickly and so hiking here is
largely a cross-country affair. I walked from the ranger station more
or less southwest across the park, passing many lakes, to the little
settlement of Angas. There are four buses a week from here to
Cuenca via Soldados, so don't rely too heavily on transport out.
Your best bet is to bring enough food for a week and just amble
round gently; you'll see very few people and the scenery is really
marvellous.

The major part of the land area is *páramo* and many typical
páramo species may be seen. Most exciting of all is perhaps the
condor which is still occasionally sighted. You will hear as well as
see the Andean snipe. Highland thickets of the dwarf quinua tree
dot the landscape and are filled with a fascinating variety of primitive plant life: the trees and ground are covered with mosses, lichens,
fungi, mushrooms, and toadstools. One of the most colourful and
common flowers is a small, bulbous, yellow and red flower known
locally as *sarazhima*. You'll see rabbits and, with luck, a white-
tailed deer or fox. The lakes are filled with trout and sport fishing
is permitted. Towards and beyond the park's western boundaries are
almost impenetrable cloud forests. There is one area of the park,
however, which is known for its accessible cloud forest: the eastern
part near Laguna Llaviuco. This is one of the very few areas of cloud
forest on the eastern slopes of the Western Cordillera. It is reached
by a short signposted dirt track leading from the main park entrance
road about a third of the way between the village of Sayausi and the
park station. Many more bird species are found here including the
grey-breasted mountain toucan (*Andigena hypoglauca*), the multi-
coloured masked trogon (*Trogon personatus*), and various tropical
woodpeckers. Another park station is being planned for this vicinity.

The altitude of the park averages around 4000 m with no areas
rising above 4500 m, hence there is no snow and the weather is
relatively mild. Even on colder nights temperatures barely dip
below freezing whilst during the day it is often sunny and warm.
Visits can be made year round although April to June are said to be
the wettest months and August and September the driest.

CHAPTER 6
THE EASTERN CORDILLERA

INTRODUCTION

This is perhaps the most interesting region for the adventurou
outdoor traveller. The Eastern Cordillera is, on average, higher ar
more massive than its western counterpart and counts amongst i
mountains the famous volcanoes of Cotopaxi, Cayambe, Antisan
El Altar, and Sangay, which rank respectively second, third, fourt
fifth, and seventh highest in the country. The last named is considere
to be the most continuously active volcano in South America, if n
the world.

The high eastern slopes of these mountains are bordered by
relatively thin strip of *páramo* which changes abruptly to almo
impenetrable high mountain cloud forest on the lower slopes befo
merging into what is commonly called 'jungle' but is in fact tl
tropical rain forest of the lowlands. Hot air masses rise up the easte
flanks of the mountains depositing enough rainfall to make the hi
mountain cloud forest the wettest part of Ecuador; indeed, wi
some areas averaging over 5000 mm of rain per year, it is one of t
wettest regions on earth. It is also extremely thickly vegetated ar
so the middle and lower slopes have been little disturbed by ma
The story is often told of the *hacienda* owner who, upon bei
asked how extensive his land was, replied, "I don't really know –
far as you can go to the east". Even today the eastern slopes are
little explored that *haciendas* with ill defined limits to the east st
exist. These are the haunts of the rarely seen mountain tapir and tl
Andean spectacled bear, the two largest land mammals in Ecuad
and considered endangered species. Their rarity is due not only
hunting and land encroachment but also to the almost impenetrab
nature of their environment – no one really knows how many
these elusive animals are left.

The mountains themselves tend to be covered with more sno
than those of the Western Cordillera because of the higher precipit
tion on the eastern slopes. The peaks are normally climbed from t
western side, partly because the heavily populated Central Valley li

on this side and partly because the eastern side is difficult to get to, often clouded in, and the summits are more heavily corniced. Adventurous climbers seeking new routes could look for eastern approaches to these mountains.

As with the Western Cordillera, the mountains of this range will be dealt with systematically from north to south; descriptions of both climbing and hiking routes will be given and walks into the rarely visited eastern slopes are also described.

Sara Urco.

CAYAMBE (5790 m)

INTRODUCTION   Cayambe, a massive extinct volcano, is located about 65 km northeast of Quito and is both Ecuador's third highest peak and the third highest peak in the Americas north of the equator. It also enjoys the distinction of being the highest point on the earth's surface through which the equator directly passes (at about 4600 m on the south side). It was first climbed in 1880 by, you guessed it, Whymper and the Carrel cousins. Although technically not very difficult it is rather dangerous due to crevasses and avalanches. In 1974 such an avalanche killed three well known Ecuadorian climbers: Jose Bergé, Carlos Oleas, and César Ruales. A well equipped refuge has been built on the southwest flanks of the mountain at 4600 m and named after the three climbers. The newest of Ecuador's refuges, it was opened in 1981 and has bunks for about forty climbers, running water, bathrooms, kitchen facilities, basic food supplies, a fireplace, a lunch room with a beautiful view (and chandeliers!), and permanent guards to look after your gear when you climb. There is a four wheel drive jeep track to the refuge and it costs between US $1 to $2 per night to stay there. Card carrying members of Ecuadorian and internationally recognized climbing clubs pay a reduced rate.
(N.B. I have heard recent reports of vandalism and absence of the hut guardian – talk to climbers in Quito for the most up to date information.)

The IGM make a 1:50,000 topographical map called Cayambe which shows part of the route to the refuge and part of the mountain. The road is too new to be mapped. The map also shows the old approach used in the days before the hut was built. The area is part of the Cayambe – Coca Ecological Reserve but there is no evidence of development.

DIRECTIONS   To get to the hut one first takes a bus to Cayambe which leaves Quito from one of the northern stations (see *Transportation* in Chapter 3). On the southern outskirts of Cayambe there is a turn off to the right from the Pan American Highway. There is no sign at present but many locals know that the road goes to Hacienda Hato (also known as H. Piemonte) and then on to the refuge. The 25 km to the refuge can normally be driven all the way if you use a four wheel drive vehicle. There are no buses but you can usually hitch as far as H. Hato (about 6 km) and further at weekends. At the *hacienda* turn left (right leads to Sara Urco) and continue until a T junction at about km 14 where there is a sign 'Reserva Natural Cayambe – Coca' where you turn left. So far the road has been cobbled all the way but a few kilometres further the cobbles stop though work is continuing slowly. There is so little traffic that midweek you'll have to walk most of the way which makes a good hiking trip even if you don't intend to climb the mountain. There are good views of the ancient lava flows of this now extinct volcano as well as of the Glaciar Hermoso (the beautiful glacier) near to the refuge.

To climb Cayambe, get as early a start as possible to take advantage of the frozen snow; later in the day the softened snow often avalanches. Head directly over the rocky hill behind the hut and climb onto the glacier on the other side; this will take about an hour. Climb more or less north up the glacier and be alert for crevasses. Some rocky outcrops, the Picos Jarrín, will be seen ahead and will be reached in another 1½ hours. From this area turn right and head east up the mountain. The glacier here is split by several large crevasses and route-finding can be a problem. Marker flags (wands) are useful. Having successfully negotiated the crevassed area you will come to the base of the final somewhat steeper snowfield below the

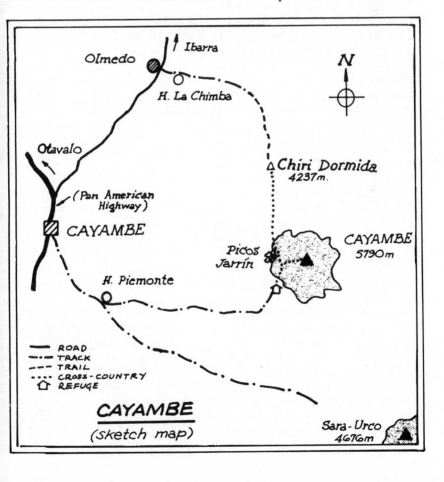

summit. This snowfield is sometimes swept by avalanches and it was here that Bergé, Ruales, and Oleas were killed. It is foolhardy to attempt to climb this unless it is still early enough in the day for the snow to be frozen. At the top, a large overhanging crevasse has made reaching the highest point somewhat difficult in recent years. Try rounding it to the left. Because of the new refuge, Cayambe is quite frequently climbed these days despite its dangerous reputation so you can sometimes follow footprints and wands from previous parties. Allow 4 to 6 hours for the ascent.

The old route avoids the refuge completely. You head for the village of Olmedo about 10 km northeast of Cayambe town. Mules and guides may be hired from Hacienda La Chimba, in Olmedo's western outskirts. It takes 5 to 8 hours to reach Chiri Dormida where water is available. Camp here. From Chiri Dormida a further 2 to 3 hours are needed to reach Picos Jarrín from where the route continues as on the new normal route. Since the construction of the refuge this route is rarely used.

Cayambe is one of the less explored of Ecuador's major peaks and new routes could be attempted by highly experienced climbers. The mountain has rarely been climbed other than by the Picos Jarrín route described.

Snow storms and high winds are more frequent on Cayambe than on many other peaks. It can be climbed year round although October through January is said to be the best period.

SARA URCO (4676 m)

With turned out toes we went cautiously along the crisp arete, sharp as a roof-top, and at 1.30 p.m. stood on the true summit of Sara-Urco; a shattered ridge of gneiss – wonder of wonders, blue sky above – strewn with fragments of quartz and micaschist . . . without a hint of vegetation.

Edward Whymper, 1892

Sara Urco is one of Ecuador's few non-volcanic peaks and lies about 15 km southeast of Cayambe peak. Despite its low altitude it is normally snow capped and so many sources and climbers believe it to be higher than the given IGM elevation. It is surrounded by jumbled up *páramo* which is either boggy or brushy and difficult to move through; hence this is not a frequently climbed mountain. It is technically straightforward and was first climbed in 1880 by Whymper and the Carrels, who seem to have got everywhere. December and January are the best climbing months; the rest of the year is wet.

Although I haven't climbed this peak I obtained the following description from various climbers in Ecuador.

Access is the same as for Cayambe as far as the Hacienda Hato (or H. Piemonte) after which you turn right (left leads to Cayambe). About 3 km beyond the *hacienda* the road peters out. Somewhere around here lives Señor Juan Farinango who is the local guide and can arrange mule hire. On the first day the guides take you in a generally southeasterly direction past an area known as La Dormida; several small rivers must be forded. The *páramo* here is known locally as *pantano* which means marsh or swamp. It takes a day to reach the Río Bolteado where camp is set up. The following day you continue in a southeasterly direction to the foot of the southwest ridge which is easy to ascend to the summit. You'll probably need to camp high on the mountain and make the summit on the third day. A glacier was still in existence in 1981.

Due to the inhospitable nature of the surroundings it is advisable to hire mules and a guide. There are no decent maps of the area available at this time.

LAS PUNTAS (4452 m) AND THE OYACACHI AREA

The name of this mountain means 'the points' and indeed Las Puntas is more like a long serrated ridge than a mountain. Some authorities have reported as many as fifty separate small peaks on the ridge which lies 30 km east of Quito. South and east of Las Puntas is a very wet lake district which eventually leads to the lowland forests. This area could well be explored by those hoping to catch a glimpse of spectacled bear or mountain tapir – but don't be too hopeful.

To get there from Quito take a No. 3 Colmena – Batán bus and get off at the El Batán roundabout. Catch an El Quinche bus at the eastern exit on the road which heads into the Oriente. The bus goes through the villages of Cumbaya, Tumbaco, Puembo, Yaruquí, Checa, and El Quinche. Get off at Checa some 1½ to 2 hours out of Quito, cross a railway line just beyond the village, and turn right on a dirt road which passes Hacienda Santa Teresita. This peters out as a track high in the *páramo*. Las Puntas is the obvious horseshoe shaped ridge in front of you to the east. The western inside of the mountain is steep and difficult to climb; head around the north side and approach via the gentler eastern slopes. It's a day's walk from Checa to the mountain so bring your camping gear.

This area can be used as a jumping off point for the adventurous traveller well-equipped with rain gear and food. South of Las Puntas is a large boggy area of dozens of lakes. You will eventually come out on the Quito–Lago Agrio road about 20 km away. A more ambitious hike would be to head to the Laguna Oyacachi a few kilometres away; it is the largest lake to the east of Las Puntas. From here follow the Río Oyacachi which drains out of the south corner of the lake and then flows eastwards towards the tiny village of Oyacachi which is about 13 crow-flying kilometres away; probably twice that on foot. The IGM 1:50,000 Oyacachi topographical map shows a trail on the north side of the river beginning about two-thirds of the way between the lake and the village and continuing into the village. From Oyacachi the trail continues eastwards down the Río Oyacachi valley, crossing the river and then heading southeast to the settlement of El Chaco on the Quito–Lago Agrio road; some 35 km as the crow flies.

I have never done this hike, nor met anyone who has, so you go at your own risk. A few general pointers – Las Puntas is over 4000 m high and El Chaco is at barely 1000 m so trying the hike in reverse would be tough, to say the least. Remember crow-flying kilometres are usually doubled in reality. The trail from Oyacachi to El Chaco will probably be in fairly good shape and your biggest problem will be finding Oyacachi. Expect rain, mud, and more rain. To see any wildlife will require determination and patience. If you want to have something to practice on, try *The Andes to the Jungle* hike on page 126.

THE ANTISANA AREA

INTRODUCTION Volcán Antisana (5704 m) is the fourth highest mountain in Ecuador, but is seldom seen by tourists because of its position some 55 km southeast of Quito well away from any main road. The broad summit contains four separate peaks which are, in descending order, the central, eastern, northeastern, and southern summits. Their elevations are widely disagreed upon. These four summits represent the highest points of a crater rim; the crater itself is totally filled with glacial ice and doesn't appear to be active. For this reason Antisana is popularly supposed to be extinct, but volcanologists claim that its comparatively recent major eruptions indicate that the volcano is, in fact, still active. The 10 km long lava flow near the Hacienda Pinantura, to the west of the mountain, is attributed to an eruption around 1760 and the 6 km long flow by Laguna Papallacta, to the north of the mountain, dates from 1773. Both these flows originated from fissures in the sides of the volcano, thus a cone is absent. Some fumarolic activity still exists near the highest summit.

The climbing history of this mountain is predictable: another first ascent by Whymper and the Carrels in 1880. Whymper wrote that he could smell sulphurous fumes during the ascent. The lower peaks however, are more of a challenge and did not see conquests until the 1970s by various Ecuadorian climbers.

The access town of Píntag, with its cobbled streets and tiled roofs, is unusually attractive and the surrounding farmland green and beautiful. The *páramo* near Antisana is more varied than usual. Flowering *puya* plants are plentiful, providing nectar for the many hummingbirds, and there are even some rather subdued looking *frailejones*. The further east or 'around the back' of the mountain you go, the more likely you are to see animals such as the white-tailed deer, mountain tapir, puma, and spectacled bear. Lava fields are a fascinating feature of this area. Antisana itself is a splendid sight with its four peaks covered with blue glaciers; to the west is Cotopaxi showing its best profile.

A jeep road runs to the foot of Antisana. Very little traffic uses this track which is in poor condition and ideal for hiking. Many people will choose to return by the same route, but it is possible to hike cross-country to Papallacta on the Quito–Lago Agrio road, or cross the *páramo* to Cotopaxi via Sincholagua.

ACCESS Buses leave Terminal Terrestre in Quito several times a day for the hour long journey to Píntag through lovely scenery and pretty villages. From Píntag head south on a cobbled road to Hacienda Pinantura (also known as Hacienda La Cocha) some 7 to 8 km away. Take the uphill road whenever you come to a fork. At one

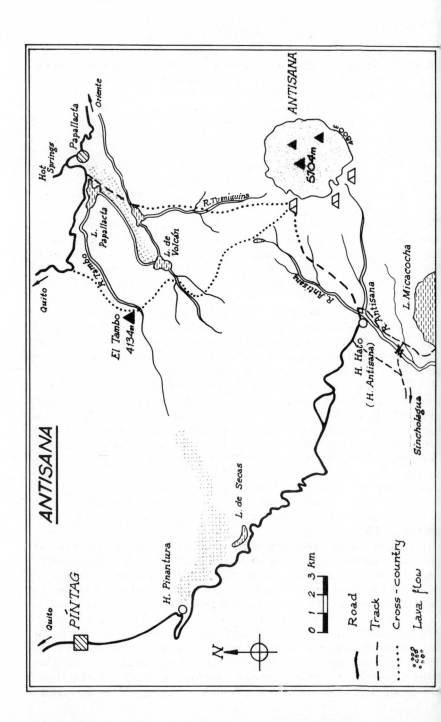

point you have a choice of three roads; take the middle one.

At the *hacienda* there is a locked gate across the road which will be unlocked upon production of a permit. This can be obtained from the Asociación de Andinismo de Pichincha in Quito, or through one of the climbing clubs. This permit is for vehicles only; if you're on foot you won't need one.

Near the *hacienda* look out for the lava field to your left which is over 200 years old and covered with moss and shrubs. You have the choice of following a path across the lava for a while, or continuing to the *hacienda* and picking up the jeep track; a longer but easier route. If you decide to cross the lava, look for a track going up what looks like piles of rubble. This track soon dwindles to a path. There are beautiful little rock gardens between the chunks of lava, and all sorts of flowers can be admired. It's worth going out of your way to find a flowering *puya* with its apple-green flowers. After about an hour of lava-leaping you will want to join the jeep track. Look out for an easy access place on your right where the lava cliff is low and no scrambling is involved. Once on the jeep track you simply keep walking, or hitch-hiking, past a string of beautiful lakes dammed by the lava flows, through various gates, and over several bridges. The cobbles have long since finished and if you're driving, four wheel drive will probably be necessary by now. Continue up the road as it twists and turns through broad fields and *páramo* and look out for short cuts if you're on foot.

About 25 km by road after Hacienda Pinantura you'll pass the Hacienda Hato (also known as Hacienda Antisana). 3 to 4 km due south is Laguna Micacocha which is famous for trout fishing. To reach the mountain turn left, or northwest, on a rapidly deteriorating track. The area is flat pastureland and looks very eerie in low evening sunlight with dozens of cattle skulls dotting the landscape. The track is driveable for about 8 km and peters out high in the *páramo* west of the mountain. From here head east for another 2 km and make your base camp as close to the snowline as possible.

THE CLIMB

Antisana is one of the more difficult peaks in Ecuador to climb and is dangerous because of the many crevasses and bad weather. The lengthy access and lack of a mountain refuge compound your problems; this is the highest peak in Ecuador with no hut, and you have to carry complete wet weather camping gear and food for several days. My attempts on the peak were unsuccessful: once because of bad weather, and once, and I blush to admit it, because after a late night of story telling around our campfire we all overslept! From the base camp the mountain has been climbed southeast to a saddle and then north to the summit. A route heading northeast and then south to the summit has also been described. A base camp is occasionally made by the southern glacier to attempt the southern peaks. Everyone agrees that the crevasses are both numerous and dangerous so this is a mountain for experienced climbers who will no doubt manage to find their own route.

HIKING TO PAPALLACTA

Hikers wishing to continue northwards to Papallacta will have to go cross-country. This is not easy as there are no paths, the countryside is rough, and the vegetation can be extremely dense, especially in the valley bottoms. From the climbers' base camp one heads roughly north, following the Río Tumiguina valley to a lake by the lava flow some 10 km away. From the right (eastern) shores of the lake you'll find the continuation of the Río Tumiguina and a faint path following it. This soon turns away from the river valley and then crosses the lava flow reaching Laguna Papallacta and the Quito–Lago Agrio road after 3 or 4 km. This is a rough trail. If you wanted to do the hike in reverse, from Papallacta to Antisana, your main problem would be to find the beginning of the rough trail across the lava flow. It begins just beyond (to the east) of Laguna Papallacta but is not very easy to find. Once on it, it is straightforward to follow it to the lake where you head south to the mountain.

I took a completely different route from the Quito–Lago Agrio road to Antisana, which took me up the Tambo river valley and across swampy pasture. Leave Quito on a bus to Papallacta, Baeza, or Lago Agrio in the lowlands. The last village before Papallacta is Pifo; soon afterwards the tarmac road changes to gravel and after some 24 km you cross a 4100 m pass where there is a statue and a national parks building (which is new and may even have someone in it by now - it didn't when I was there). About 6 km after the pass and 8 km before Papallacta you reach a sharp hairpin bend followed by two small bridges next to one another. There are good views of Laguna Papallacta about 3 km to the east. Get off the bus here. To your right is the Río Tambo valley, but don't expect the trail marked on IGM maps towards the Hacienda El Tambo to exist.

Head southwest up the Tambo river valley for 4 to 5 km until you reach the long flat-topped hill called El Tambo (4134 m). By now you should be on the opposite (eastern) bank of the Río Tambo – it's easy to jump or ford – and you head over a shallow pass to the southeast of El Tambo. Continuing in a southeasterly direction over boggy countryside for a couple of kilometres will bring you within sight of Laguna de Volcán. From here you head vaguely south, though some very steep sections will force you to detour. About 5 km south of Laguna de Volcán you'll find a long hill with several high peaks along it which you skirt to your left (east). You'll come to a small swampy lake with many semi-wild horses nearby. From this (unnamed) lake head southeast for 2 to 3 km to the base camp area.

These are both challenging and interesting routes and require maps, compass, and route-finding ability.

Papallacta, some 3 km beyond the lake to the east, has a small, basic hotel and restaurants. Just before the village there is a sign to the left which indicates the kilometre long road to the thermal hot springs. There are a couple of pools and changing rooms but the area is little visited – you may well have it to yourselves midweek. They are the best hot springs I've found in Ecuador. You could probably camp next to them (slip the caretaker a few sucres). The views can be superb.

HIKING TO COTOPAXI

One more possible hike from Antisana is the 2 or 3 day trip southeast towards Volcáns Sincholagua and Cotopaxi. From the Antisana base camp retrace your steps to Hacienda Hato and head due south to Laguna Micacocha which is 2 hours from the *hacienda* and reputed to have good fishing. Go due west from the lake to Sincholagua and beyond this mountain meet the jeep track joining Cotopaxi in the south with Quito in the north. I haven't tried this walk, but it's reported to be fairly straightforward.

For all these hikes you'll need a compass and maps. Get the IGM 1:50,000 Píntag and Sincholagua topographical sheets. The adjoining maps to the east are, at the present time, only planametric, but you can buy three topographical maps of the 1:25,000 series instead: the Papallacta, Antisana, and Laguna de Micacocha sheets, although the different scales make them a little confusing.

The weather is generally wet and cold. If your tent and raingear aren't waterproof you'll probably be miserable. And if you think they are waterproof you'll know for sure by the end of your hike. With Oriente weather conditions prevailing, the driest months are November through February; the wettest months are June through August.

Don't forget a stove as there's little firewood. What there is looks better on the ground than up in smoke.

CHE–G

COTOPAXI NATIONAL PARK AND SURROUNDINGS

Cotopaxi's shape is the most beautiful and regular of all the colossal peaks in the high Andes. It is a perfect cone covered by a thick blanket of snow which shines so brilliantly at sunset it seems detached from the azure of the sky.

Alexander von Humboldt, 1802.

INTRODUCTION   The Galapagos Islands excepted, this is without a doubt Ecuador's showpiece national park. It has an administrative centre, museum, and wardens within its borders – luxuries rarely found in other parks. There are picnic areas, camping sites, huts, and a mountain refuge, making it somewhat similar to the national parks in North America and Europe.

The centrepiece of the park is Volcán Cotopaxi (5897 m) which lies about 55 km south of Quito and whose symmetrical cone can often be seen from the capital on a clear day. This active volcano is Ecuador's second highest mountain and it has long been considered the highest active volcano in the world (although recent claims in favour of Tupungato on the Argentine–Chilean border cannot be discounted).

The history of Cotopaxi's activity is the most dramatic in Ecuador. Although other volcanoes may be more active geologically, Cotopaxi has caused the most death and destruction. Records of its eruptions date back to 1534 though it was undoubtedly active long before then. After a long period of dormancy, Cotopaxi erupted three times in 1742, destroying the town of Latacunga and killing hundreds of people and livestock. More eruptions followed in 1743, 1744, and 1766. A major eruption in 1768 again destroyed Latacunga, which had been rebuilt, and there was much loss of life and property. Almost a century of inactivity followed, but in 1853 Cotopaxi again began to display its awesome power and continued erupting frequently for several years. Four separate eruptions occurred in 1877 and the one of the 26th of June produced catastrophic lahars (avalanches of ice, snow, water, mud, and rocks), one of which reached Esmeraldas on the Pacific coast, and another which swept down on ill-fated Latacunga, wiping out the greater part of it yet again. This lahar was recorded as having reached the town in 30 minutes. Latacunga lies 35 km southwest of Cotopaxi as the crow flies but the lahar would have followed the lie of the land by a more circuitous route – the concept of a huge wall of volcanic and glacial debris sweeping toward one at some 90 km per hour, or 25 m per second, is impossible to comprehend. As Michael Andrews remarks in *The Flight of the Condor*, "I find it very curious that Latacunga has been rebuilt repeatedly on its old site." Frequent but minor eruptions continued for 8 years after this catastrophe. Since 1885 eruptions have been limited to two minor ones in 1903 and 1904, and a disputed one in 1942. Fumarolic activity continues in Cotopaxi's crater at present, as anyone who has climbed the volcano will know.

Cotopaxi was first climbed in 1872 from the southwest by the German geologist Wilhelm Reiss accompanied by Angel M. Escobar, a Colombian. A few months later the German, Stübel, accompanied by four Ecuadorians (Jantui, Páez, Ramón, and Rodriguez) logged the first Ecuadorian ascent. Edward Whymper with the Carrel cousins spent a night on the summit in 1880 – a somewhat hazardous exercise bearing in mind the restless nature of the volcano at that time. Since then many successful ascents have been made and today the mountain is a popular destination for weekend mountaineers and tourists from Quito as well as foreign climbers. Despite its relative simplicity this is not a climb for the inexperienced, and beginners should avail themselves of professional guides.

The national park surrounding the volcano offers excellent hiking and camping opportunities as well as lesser peaks to climb. Rumiñahui (4712 m) and Morurco (c. 4840 m) lie within the park boundaries and the peaks of Sincholagua (4893 m) and Quilindaña (4878 m) are found just outside the park. There is talk of extending the park boundaries. Hiking a complete circuit around the base of Cotopaxi is a good 6 to 7 day trip and all the above peaks can be seen or climbed.

ACCESS   This describes two ways to reach the administrative centre. Hiking or climbing routes from there are described individually.

There are two entrance roads to the park, both of which start from the Pan American Highway and are therefore accessible by any Quito–Latacunga bus. The first entrance is at the old NASA minitrak station, about 13 km to the south of Machachi. The satellite tracking station has recently suspended operations but the turn off is still marked with a huge sign and the tracking equipment is plainly visible. About 5 to 6 km further south on the Pan American is another turn off with a small (blue) sign. Both entrances are frequently used and during the weekend there is little difficulty in hitch-hiking into the park but midweek there is almost no traffic.

The first turn off is asphalted for the first 2 km until it reaches the old tracking station where it becomes a dirt road. There are signs most of the way; you pass a railway station and then cross the tracks and continue to the Río Daule campsite which is about 7 km beyond the tracking stations. This campsite has plenty of flat tent spaces, two small picnic shelters (unsuitable for sleeping in), and fireplaces.

Drinking water is from the river about 100 m past the campsite, beyond a bend in the road. If on foot, this is a good place to spend your first night.

The dirt road continues climbing slowly and 1 to 2 km beyond Río Daule passes a hairpin bend with a camp by it; there is a stable and a thatched hut, but no water. After a further 1 to 2 km take an unmarked left hand turn (look for herds of llamas; the animals are being studied in the area) down a road which continues through an entrance gate arriving 4 to 5 km further on at the administration centre. Here there is a small museum with stuffed animals and birds, including a condor. This is useful for identifying animals which you may see in the park. There are maps and posters (though none for sale) and verbal information is obtainable. It is about 15 km from this centre, Campamento Mariscal Sucre, to the climbers' refuge.

To reach Campamento Mariscal Sucre from the second entrance road head 5 to 6 km further south on the Pan American to a turn off marked by a small blue 'Parque Nacional Cotopaxi' sign. About a kilometre beyond the turn off is a small, rounded, grassy hill on the left; this useful landmark is reputedly a preconquest mound but no one seems to know very much about it. Take the entrance road and immediately cross the railway tracks. Ignore a right turn soon after the tracks and go about a kilometre to a T junction where you take the right fork. A few hundred metres further take a sharp left turn and continue towards the park on a road which has signs where necessary. You meet up with the first entrance road by the park entrance gate and continue to the administration centre. This is about a 15 km trip from the Pan American Highway.

If you're on foot you can arrive anytime but if you're driving remember that the entrance station is open only from 8 a.m. – 12 noon and from 2 p.m.–6 p.m. During weekends it is open longer; from 7 a.m.–12 noon and from 2 p.m.–6.30 p.m. Outside of these hours you must find someone to open the locked gate. You'll need your passport and a small fee is charged.

HIKING AROUND COTOPAXI
This is a beautiful and not too difficult hike which takes about a week and can be combined with ascents of some of the nearby peaks. A dirt road runs more than halfway around the volcano but some cross-country hiking will be involved to complete the circuit. Good maps are available from the IGM; the 1:50,000 topographical sheets of Machachi, Sincholagua, Cotopaxi, and Mulaló will be required. If you're a beginner and not confident of your abilities to hike without trails, you can do the dirt road sections and return the way you came. During weekends you will be able to hitch-hike much of the way but midweek you will probably find the jeep road deserted.

Your first step is to reach the administrative centre at Campamento Mariscal Sucre by one of the two entrance roads described in *Access*. If you are on foot your first night's camp will probably be at Río Daule. On the second day you should reach the administration centre in 4 to 6 hours from Río Daule and, after visiting the museum, can continue to one of the several nearby campsites.

The first campsite is some 2 to 3 km along the road beyond Campamento Mariscal Sucre. There is a small sign and a turn off to the left onto a small plain where there are little picnic shelters, an outhouse, a recently built cabin, and water running from a pipe in the gully behind the campsite. On a clear day there are excellent views of Chimborazo about 100 km to the south southwest. This campsite provides one base for climbing Rumiñahui but don't leave your gear here because it is not safe.

About a kilometre further down the road is a second camping site, also signed, but this time to the right. Again picnic shelters and a small cabin are available, but there is no running water.

Just beyond the turn off to the second campsite there is a track off to the left of the road across a large plain to Laguna de Limpios (also known as Limpiopungo) at about 3800 m. Around the lake you should watch for waterfowl and other birds, as well as the black *Atelopus* toad (see *Natural History* in Chapter 3). There is a trail around the back of the lake which will be described in *Climbing Rumiñahui*.

To continue your hike around Cotopaxi go from the campsites, past Laguna Limpiopungo, and along the road as it begins to curve further east around the mountain. Some 2 to 3 km beyond the lake, the hiker will see a signed road to the right leading to the Cotopaxi climbers' refuge some 9 km away (see *Climbing Cotopaxi*).

About 3 km after the turn off for the refuge the road forks. The track going straight on will eventually bring you to Machachi over 20 km away to the northwest. Take the right fork and curve northeast, east, and southeast until you cross a small bridge over an unnamed river about an hour's walk beyond the fork. This point is about 8 km from the lake and you could camp here, although it is rather exposed. It's better to continue southeast a further 8 km on the gently climbing road around Cotopaxi to the next running water which is usually at the stream crossing the road just above the area marked Mudadero on the IGM map. If this fails, head left or west across flat pastureland to the Río Hualpaloma which runs all year. This camp gives good views of the northeastern flanks of Cotopaxi.

(N.B. The bridge mentioned in the above paragraph is the departure point for climbing Sincholagua.)

From this camp continue on the jeep road southeast and then south for about 7 km to the point where (on the IGM map) the road stops and becomes a four wheel drive jeep track heading east. This place is easily identified because the track makes a hairpin bend into a small but steep-walled canyon. Continue into the canyon and you'll soon come to the Río Tamboyacu; good camping is also possible here.

Now you have two choices. You can continue along the jeep road as it curves east, south, and finally back west to Hacienda El Tambo, which is the furthest driveable point and about 14 km away. At about the halfway point there is a fork where you go right. Alternatively, you can forsake the jeep track and head south across country. With the IGM maps and a compass this is quite easy. Head more or less south and pass a small conical hill (Chiguilasín Chico) to your left. Continue south across a plain (you should find a horse track) over a pass to the left of a flat-topped hill (4222 m on the map). On the other side of the pass you look down on the valley of the northwest arm of the Río Tambo. Follow the valley on the right hand side southwards for about 1½ km until you come to a large valley on your right. Here there are good views of Morurco (c. 4840 m) about 7 km to the west.

(Climbers' Note: Morurco can be approached from this area using an IGM map. Koerner (1976) writes that Morurco is a minor southern peak of Cotopaxi, has only been climbed once, and is reputed to be easy but interesting, with technical possibilities. Access is from the east and north around Cotopaxi. The snow cover is variable.)

At this point turn to the southeast and follow the Río Tambo valley for about 5 km. This valley has wonderful views of Cotopaxi behind and Quilindaña ahead and you can camp anywhere. When you get to the mouth of the valley you will see a snow-capped peak about 40 km to the northeast; this is Antisana.

At the mouth of the valley cross the southwestern arm of the Río Tambo – it is not difficult to ford. The IGM map shows a trail running along the river northeast for about 3 to 4 km to the Hacienda El Tambo, and southwest for about 16 km to the Hacienda Baños. At best this trail is no more than a meandering animal track, but the Río Tambo valley is easy enough to follow. This area is used as a base for climbs of Quilindaña (see page 109).

Heading southwest you will see a mountain with a steep rock face about 7 km away. The trail, or what you can find of it, follows the Río Tambo for 4 to 5 km, and when the river turns northwest to its headwaters, the trail continues southwest and passes this steep faced mountain (identified by its altitude of 4288 m on the map) to the right or north. Here the trail becomes quite visible and easy to follow over the pass to the north of peak 4288. Just before the pass is a large flat area which would be the best place for a last camp.

Beyond the pass north of peak 4288 the trail continues clearly to the southwest for 1 to 2 km and then joins a dirt road. This is marked only as a footpath on the IGM map. Turn left and after some 8 to 10 km you'll reach Hacienda Chalupa, which can be used as a base camp for Quilindaña. The right turn takes you out to the Pan

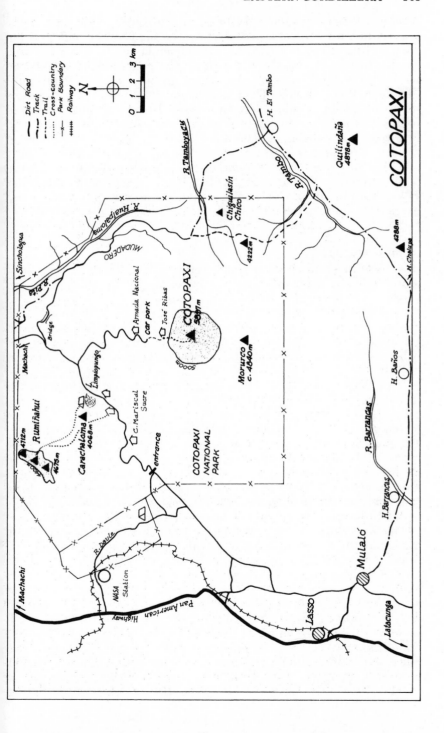

American Highway. The IGM maps are not very useful here as the road is not properly marked. Follow the road for some 7 to 8 km past a white stone block marker for Hacienda Baños. A few hundred metres further on take a left fork and after another few hundred metres go straight at a junction. There are no more major turns for the next 3 to 4 hours. Then you descend into the Río Barrancas valley where you could camp. Otherwise climb up the other side and follow the trail another 3 to 4 hours into Mulaló, where you will find buses to Latacunga. There are many forks in the trail beyond the Río Barrancas; take the most used looking trail and ask the many inhabitants for the way to Mulaló. It is possible to walk out on the road to Mulaló in one long, hard day; otherwise camp in the flat valley bottom of Río Barrancas. There are no hotels in Mulaló and buses stop running before nightfall.

CLIMBING COTOPAXI (5897 m)

If you are a mountaineering party and want to reach the climbers' refuge quickly you'll need to hire a jeep or pickup truck. This can be done in Latacunga (about 35 km southwest of the peak). Go to Plaza de Salta where you will find an *estacionamento* where there are various transportation companies. A company which will do the trip for around US $4 per pickup truck is Cooperativa de Transportes Riberas del Cutuchi. One of their drivers is Manuel Rodriguez (*carro* 22).

If you have your own vehicle or are on foot, follow directions in the *Access* and *Hiking Around Cotopaxi* sections until you get to the turn off for the climbers' refuge. The turn off is at 3830 m; it is 8½ km to the parking area at 4600 m so you have to climb hard. The road is easy to follow; en route you pass the Armada Nacional refuge at 4400 m. It's old, small, damaged, and rarely used. If you're on foot, the gully behind this refuge offers a short cut to the new refuge; it takes at least an hour with a pack. From the parking lot a trail leads up the sand to the new refuge. Though it looks very near, with a heavy pack it will take at least half an hour to walk there.

The José Ribas refuge was built in 1971 and extended in 1977. It has about three dozen bunkbeds and floor space, basic food supplies, running water, kitchen facilities, outhouses, a fireplace, and lock-up facilities for your gear when you climb. It costs about US $2 per night to stay here and card-carrying members of internationally recognized climbing clubs are given a discount.

The standard route (other routes are rarely climbed) takes 5 to 9 hours for the ascent and 2 to 4 for the descent. The snow becomes unpleasantly wet and soft by early afternoon so you should leave the hut between 12 midnight and 3 a.m. The first hour of the climb takes you up a triangular scree slope which is sometimes snow covered. Climbing onto the glacier is the most difficult part of the ascent although you can do it from several points; just left of the apex of the scree slope is one frequently used. Once you are on the glacier you climb straight up and then towards the right. There is talk of 'subtle ridges' in some accounts, but in fact the climb is rather featureless and mainly a long snow plod once the problem of getting onto the glacier has been overcome. Although the mountain is well crevassed, for the most part the crevasses are spectacularly large and open and thus easy to avoid. A route is usually well marked around the crevasses with wands and footprints – remember this is the most popular high climb in Ecuador. The main feature to look for is a huge rock face called Yanasacha (literally 'large black rock' in Quechua). You pass to the right of this and then come back to the left to reach the summit crater. The last 200 m or so are quite steep.

The classic round crater is over half a kilometre wide and a circuit is possible. Steam can be seen escaping from vents in the centre and from the walls. Expeditions into the crater have been undertaken; the first was in 1972 when a Polish–Czech expedition spent 6 hours in the crater and since then several Ecuadorians have repeated the venture.

An alternative route is occasionally used. Begin as if for the standard route, but once on the glacier below Yanasacha head left instead of right. This route is not reported to be very difficult.

Ropes, ice axes, and crampons are, of course, necessary, and a second tool for getting onto the glacier is useful. Experienced teams don't usually bother with protection, but less experienced climbers could use snow stakes, deadmen, or long ice screws.

The Cotopaxi area is blessed with the highest number of clear days per year in the Ecuadorian Andes and thus climbs may be attempted year round. Cotopaxi is further west than Cayambe and Antisana, so it experiences the climate of the central highlands rather than the Oriente. June and July are the driest months.

CLIMBING RUMIÑAHUI (4712 m)
A geologist would place Rumiñahui in Chapter 4, The Central Valley, but I include it here because it is within the confines of Cotopaxi National Park. This long-extinct volcano is located 45 km south of Quito and only 13 km northwest of Cotopaxi. It is an easy ascent and has often been climbed; surprisingly, I could find no records of ascents prior to the 1950s. Although occasionally sprinkled with snow, it is normally a walk up with a rocky scramble at the top.

Rumiñahui is named after one of Atahualpa's famous generals and means 'face of stone'. Despite the name, one should remember that the stone is heavily laced with metal, so you should descend if an electric storm threatens.

The most well-known route begins from Laguna Limpiopungo

(see *Access* and *Hiking Around Cotopaxi*). The lake is scummy but you'll find a path going around its east side and past a boggy area to the north. About a kilometre northwest of the lake you'll find possible camping spots with clean running water. This is not an officially designated campsite and has no facilities.

From here head west up a small steep-sided valley, following the stream around to the northwest to a boggy plain below the mountain. Skirt this plain to the north and cross a grassy ridge coming off the Central Summit. Once across the ridge swing west and head for the Central Summit. You'll find several wide 'ledges' traversing north to the main summit. Follow these until you come to the last major gully of reddish sand which is the route to the summit ridge. This gully is just before the large rockface at the northern end of the mountain. Climb to the top of the summit ridge, cross it, and then drop down the western wide. From here you should be able to scramble to the summit; ascents from the eastern side are difficult. Except for the last few metres, which are the usual rotten rock, the ascent is an easy scramble. Even if you don't quite make the top the view is great.

The lake, river valley, plain, and grassy ridge mentioned in the description are all quite easy to find on the IGM maps (1:50,000 series) Machachi and Sincholagua. The positions of the West and Central Summits are inaccurately marked on the IGM maps. From a mountaineer's point of view, the West Peak is the 4675 m one at map reference 770346 (Machachi), and the Central Peak is at 775352.

You may prefer to camp at the official site on the left hand side of the road about 2½ km in from the entrance station. The route from here lies up the gully behind (north of) the campsite, over the hill called Carachaloma (4068 m) which is about 1½ km to the north and then northwest up the stream valley to the boggy plain mentioned in the standard approach. This way is rather longer. The climb takes 4 to 8 hours depending on how well you've acclimatized.

Other approaches and routes are possible but less frequently climbed. Approaches are made from the northeast over the Filo Santo Domingo to the bottom of the last sandy gully described in the standard route. The rockface just north of this gully offers a technical rock route which was first climbed in 1972 by the Ecuadorian climbers Cruz, Reinoso, and Bergé. Ascents from the Machachi side (from the northwest) are reportedly possible.

CLIMBING SINCHOLAGUA (4893 m)

Sincholagua is an extinct volcano located 45 km south southeast of Quito and 17 km northeast of Cotopaxi, just outside of the national park boundary. It is one of the many mountains first ascended by Edward Whymper and the Carrels in 1880. They climbed the northwest ridge and this is still considered the normal route. It used to be

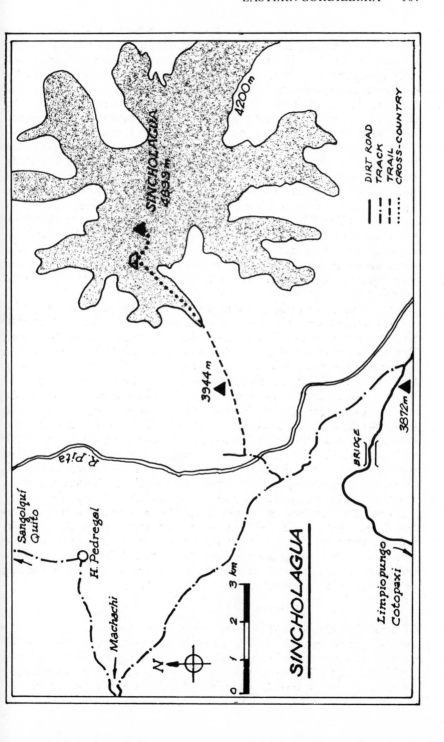

SINCHOLAGUA

a well glaciated mountain and the IGM 1:50,000 Sincholagua map shows a permanent ice cap over 1½ km long. In common with other Ecuadorian peaks the permanent snow line has receded over recent decades and today there is no permanent glacier, although after a heavy storm there is some snow cover. The climb is mainly a scramble but the summit pinnacle is of rotten rock which is loose and difficult except after a good snowfall and cold night when the rocks should be solidly frozen together.

Access is most frequently made from the south via Cotopaxi National Park although access from Quito is also possible. Enter the national park as usual and continue around Cotopaxi on the dirt road described in *Hiking Around Cotopaxi*. Go to that point on the road where you cross an unnamed river on a small bridge (map reference 865347). If in a jeep continue beyond the bridge about 3 km until you pass a perfectly cone shaped hill (3872 m) on your right and a hillock to your left. Look for an unmarked jeep trail which goes hard left and northwest. Follow this track for about 4 to 5 km, then turn right on a side track which fords the Río Pita. If on foot you can go north cross-country from the bridge and meet the track just before the right turn about 2 km north of the bridge.

This point can be reached by four wheel drive jeep from Quito. Head south on the Valle de los Chillos freeway to Sangolquí and continue to the village of Selva Alegre. Head south towards Hacienda Patichupamba and continue south towards the Río Pita and Sincholagua. The road is difficult and unsigned so ask everyone you meet for directions. It's 50 to 60 km by bad road from Selva Alegre.

Once you've crossed the Río Pita head northeast up a ridge with vehicle tracks on it, past a survey marker (3944 m), until you meet a ridge running northwest. This will take a half day on foot from the river, but a four wheel drive vehicle will get most of the way. Camp is usually made near the junction of the two ridges in order to make an early start the next day, whilst the rocks are still frozen together. Water is usually available.

From the camp continue up the northwest ridge. There are several peaks. Pass to the right of the second to last one and at the main summit beware of rockfall. After a cold or snowy night the rocks are usually frozen together but otherwise the last few metres are difficult because of the extremely rotten rock. A descent by rappelling off the summit is sometimes made.

This is the twelfth highest peak in Ecuador but is rarely visited because climbers tend to concentrate on the ten peaks over 5000 m. So much the better! In common with Rumiñahui and Cotopaxi the weather is better than average; the driest months are June through August.

CLIMBING QUILINDAÑA (4878 m)

This extinct volcano lies just outside the park boundaries about 16 km southeast of Cotopaxi and 65 km south southeast of Quito. It is an infrequently climbed, difficult, and technical mountain which was first climbed in 1952 by a large party of Ecuadorians, Colombians, French, and Italians.

The normal base for the climb is the Hacienda El Tambo (map ref. 980199 on the IGM 1:50,000 Cotopaxi map). This can be reached on foot or by four wheel drive vehicle as described in *Hiking Around Cotopaxi.* From the *hacienda* go more or less south to a saddle on the west side of the mountain. Camp is usually made just beyond the saddle at a small unnamed lake below the west face. A half day is needed from the *hacienda.* An alternative access is from the Hacienda Chalupas, which can also be reached by four wheel drive vehicle. The dirt road from Mulaló to the *hacienda* is not marked on the IGM maps so you have to get directions from everyone you meet along the way. From this *hacienda* hike north for about half a day to the lake mentioned above.

There are three routes described by Koerner and as I don't even pretend to be a rockclimber, I shall unashamedly quote him: "On the north face you will see two large and rather triangular rock faces. Somewhere, there exists an aid route which ascends here. To the left is a couloir in which runs another route that is roughly class five, but requires only four to eight pitons.

The west face may be climbed also. From the ridge to the south of the lakes, go up any one of a number of small snow gullies to a bit of a snow field. Climb this to the saddle and then go left up the summit ridge to the summit."

(Author's Note: Remember that changing snow conditions in Ecuador mean that most of the snow described above has disappeared.)

THE LLANGANATES

If you've heard of the Llanganates you've probably heard of treasure. From the time of the *conquistadores* it has been believed that treasure was buried here. The story is that when the last Inca, Atahualpa, was murdered by Pizarro, Atahualpa's general, Rumiñahui, hid the treasure from the Spaniards. Many eminent people have been convinced of its existence or have gone to look for it; they include the botanist Richard Spruce, the scientist and evolutionist Alfred Russel Wallace, George Dyott – the man who looked for Colonel Fawcett – and the British climbers Joe Brown and Hamish MacInnes. No one has found the treasure yet but a Swiss-German resident of Quito, Eugene Brunner, has looked for the treasure for almost half a century. He is convinced that he has found its location and the last I heard was that he had organized yet another major expedition (involving the Ecuadorian armed forces) to recover the gold – estimated at 750 tons!! *Vamos a ver!*

If you want to look for the treasure yourself, you'll probably find it the most difficult trip of your life. The following description by Koerner in his *The Fool's Climbing Guide to Ecuador* (which the author freely admits to being a work of fiction and plagiarism!) explains why. I like the succinctness of his description so much that I reprint it here.

"The Llanganates are a mysterious and almost impenetrable range to the northeast of Baños. Part of Atahualpa's gold is said to be hidden there, and people occasionally go off to look for it. You can too if your interest is to get hideously and hopelessly lost in 15 foot high, razor sharp pampas grass and continuous rain.

"The Llanganates also contain El Hermoso, 4571 m, an occasional snow peak, the identity of which will baffle you when first you see it from some other peak."

THE BAÑOS AREA

My room overlooks a volcano.
The window of my room overlooks a volcano.
At last a volcano.
I am two steps off from a volcano.
On our property there was a volcano.
It's my music for this evening.

Henri Michaux, 1928.

INTRODUCTION   This resort town is popular for its thermal springs, splendid scenery, and pleasant climate. Several day hikes can be made and the town is a good base for climbing Volcán Tungurahua and El Altar, as well as being the beginning of one of Ecuador's principal roads into the jungle.

The town's tourist attractions include two thermal baths (*piscinas*), a small museum, a zoo of Ecuadorian animals, and restaurants serving the typical Andean delicacy *cuy* or roast guinea pig. Your hotel manager can direct you to all of these.

By strolling down the main street in the morning, you'll see the shop-keepers busy making taffy. A glob of the soft mixture is slung onto a wooden hook on the wall, then pulled repeatedly until it hardens. Although you can buy it in bars, it's much nicer to pay a sucre for a wispy piece of still warm taffy.

Two hotels can be especially recommended to climbers and hikers. Pensión Patty at Eloy Alfaro 554 (less than two blocks from the market) is simple but very clean, friendly, family-run, and inexpensive. Cooking facilities are available and many gringos looking for hiking or climbing partners stay here. The landlady's sons, Carlos and José, are both climbers and will give advice and sometimes act as guides during their college vacations. Relatively luxurious and more expensive accommodation is available at the Hotel Sangay next to the Metropolitan Thermal Bath. Brian Warmington, the English manager, is also a climber and an expert on the area, although he is no longer able to arrange expeditions. Squash courts, swimming pool, bar, etc. are available here.

DAY HIKES FROM BAÑOS

Baños lies at 1800 m in the valley of Río Pastaza which flows from west to east. Good day hikes may be made in the mountains to the north and in the foothills of Tungurahua to the south of Baños, as well as down the river valley to the east.

To reach the steep hills on the north side of town you must cross the Río Pastaza on one of two bridges, the Puente San Francisco or the Puente San Martín. But once on the other side, directions become meaningless. There are so many paths to choose from, it's up to you how high and far you climb. Just plan to cross one bridge going and the other coming back for variety. The trail to Puente San Francisco leaves from behind the sugar cane stalls by the main bus station, and after crossing the bridge becomes very steep. You can climb to the top of the hill but the trails peter out near the summit. On a clear day you are rewarded with marvellous views of Tungurahua and Chimborazo, as well as of green cultivated fields, passion flowers, waterfalls, and the turbulent Río Pastaza.

The Puente San Martín lies over a kilometre west of town. Walk out on the main west-bound road, cross a bridge, and keep going until you reach a right fork by a blue religious shrine just before the police checkpoint. Take this fork and walk less than a kilometre to the bridge. It crosses an impressive gorge and a few hundred metres to the right is the waterfall known as Cascada Ines María which can be seen if you take a rough trail to the right from near the bridge. The dirt road continues a few kilometres to the village of Lligua and at several points trails climb the hill to the right of the road so you can take your pick.

If you prefer a day hike with clearer directions and well defined trails then head for the hills south of town. The hike to Pondoa on the slopes of Volcán Tungurahua is one idea (see *Tungurahua*). Another possibility is the hike to the village of Runtun, which consists of half a dozen buildings, one of which is a bar with a pool table! There are two trails to Runtun; the shorter of the two will take about 2 hours from Baños. Leave town by heading south on Calle 6 (Calle Thomas Halflantes) which soon passes Escuela Vicente Maldonado. Just beyond the school the road becomes a footpath which climbs diagonally left up the hill towards a house with a huge cross plainly visible on the sky line. It's the only good trail so you can't miss it. It will take about an hour to reach the cross with excellent views of Baños. The trail now doubles back to the right and towards the top of the hill until it reaches Runtun. Immediately before the village there is a fork; the left goes to the village (50 m) and the right goes down to Baños. This alternative descent is rather longer than returning the way you came. On a clear day the views of Tungurahua from near Runtun are magnificent.

Finally, if you've had enough of running up and down steep mountain sides, you can walk, hitch, or take a bus (marked Agoyan) as far as you like on the road towards the Oriente. There are three major landmarks which are accessible in a day from Baños. Some 2 km from the town centre is San Vicente where there's a small zoo. It houses an interesting collection of Ecuadorian species including the rare harpy eagle. The zoo keeper is interested in his job and will give you plenty of information and perhaps let you into some of the cages for photography.

Once your zoo visit has been concluded you can continue about
6 km to the famous Agoyan Falls (where the bus terminates). The
falls are visible from the road and you can then continue walking or
hitching a further 10 km to the Río Verde Falls. There are many
different cascades along the road, but the ones at Río Verde are the
most impressive. The views along the road are wonderful as the steep
walled Río Pastaza canyon slowly opens up into the Oriente. Once
at the little village of Río Verde, walk through town and over the
road bridge until you find a trail to your right, just by the last house
in town. The trail leads steeply down to the Río Pastaza which is
crossed by a suspension footbridge from where you can view the
falls. Better still scramble right up to them on the steep and narrow
path immediately before the footbridge. It is an exciting place;
the constricted gorge reverberates with power and it is difficult to

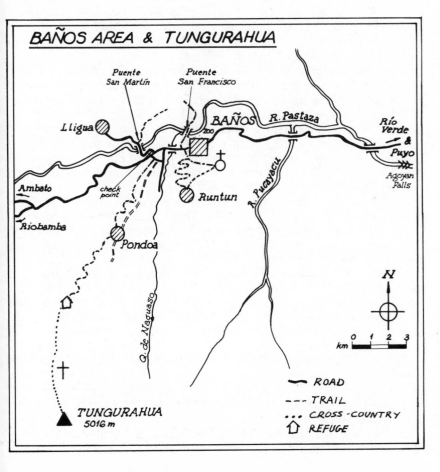

make yourself heard above the roar. This point is 20 km from Baños and about as far as you can easily reach in a day and hitch back to Baños – further trips into the jungle are included in the Oriente section.

TUNGURAHUA (5016 m)

Tungurahua is a beautiful and active snow-capped volcano situated about 10 km south of Baños. An eruption in 1777 destroyed several towns and a major eruption was recorded early this century. Present activity is limited to a few fumaroles and steam vents, and is responsible for the natural hot springs found in Baños. The volcano was first climbed in 1873 by the Germans, Wilhelm Reiss and Alfons Stübel.

From a climber's point of view, Tungurahua is rather an anomaly. It has been described both as 'easy to access and to climb' and also 'one of the hardest climbs in Ecuador'. Both descriptions are correct because although the climb is straightforward and easy from a technical viewpoint, it is physically demanding as it involves 3200 m of vertical ascent from Baños at 1800 m.

Start your climb at the western entrance to Baños at a police checkpoint. Across the highway you'll see a dirt road bearing up and to the right. Walk up this road about 100 m and turn right at a sign for Refugio Nicolás Martínez. A road is being constructed up towards the refuge; it will replace the trail which is very steep and narrow. It follows a ridge with fine views of Baños and 1 or 2 hours walking are needed to reach the small village of Pondoa. Stop at the Pondoa store and buy a ticket to use the hut facilities (less than a dollar). The owner of the store will also tell you how to reach the hut and can introduce you to the local guide, Sr. Angel Perez who has climbed the volcano dozens of times and is very experienced. He doesn't have much equipment to rent but can arrange mule hire and guide you if you wish. Only very basic supplies (beer, sardines, and crackers) are available at the store.

It takes 4 to 6 hours to climb from Pondoa to the refuge. The trail is marked by paint splashes or stakes. There are many side trails which usually peter out quickly so if you get lost retrace your footsteps to the main trail which is not very difficult to follow. At several points the trail goes through 'tunnels' of bamboo and other tropical vegetation.

When you reach the refuge (built in the late 1970's) you will find floor space for about eighteen people and a propane cooking stove. Water is obtained from a spring about 200 m beyond the hut. The altitude here is about 3800 m and the view of Chimborazo's east face is impressive.

The climb from the hut to the top is best attempted in the early morning before the summit snow becomes soft and slushy. A dawn start is adequate. Head south southeast to a survey marker at about 4000 m. About 1 or 2 hours above the hut a rockband is reached through which you can easily scramble and soon after you pass an aluminium cross. Here bear a little to the right (south) towards the craters which will take about 2 more hours to reach.

There are two craters but only the smaller one is presently active. Climbers sometimes camp in here because it is well sheltered – but don't get too close to the steam vents. The inactive south crater is larger and has a more typical crater shape with beautifully coloured rock walls.

About 45 minutes are needed to climb from the craters to the highest point. Walk straight up the snowfield between the craters. Crampons and ice axe are all that are needed as there is no major crevasse danger and the slope is gentle. Indeed, experienced climbers have reached the top merely by kicking snowsteps with their boots. The top is rather featureless, so if there is any hint of fog take compass bearings.

WARNING: This is perhaps the easiest snow climb in Ecuador and it is very tempting for beginning climbers to attempt this 5000 m peak. Enough time must be spent acclimatizing in Quito before the climb, as the low altitude of Baños is not sufficient for acclimatization. The apparent simplicity of this climb can fool you – remember climbers have died on Tungurahua.

EL ALTAR (5319 m)

INTRODUCTION   This, the fifth highest mountain in Ecuador, undoubtedly involves the most technical climbing and has one of the longest approaches. Situated some 170 km south of Quito, El Altar is an extinct volcano which at one time was probably higher than Cotopaxi, but a huge ancient eruption almost totally destroyed the cone leaving a steep-sided and jagged crater, 3 km in diameter. The west wall was destroyed, allowing easy access into the crater but the volcano has never been climbed from within. Despite repeated attempts by many climbers, including Whymper, the icy ramparts of El Altar withstood all assaults until July 7 1963, when an Italian expedition led by Marino Tremonti conquered the last unclimbed 5000 m mountain in Ecuador.

Indian legend dates the huge final explosion to 1460, but volcanologists agree that it must have been far more ancient. Today, the volcano is inactive. Nine separate sub-summits are recognised on its reversed C shaped crater. They have now all been climbed, although one of the Frailes was not conquered until 1979 by a team of six Ecuadorian climbers led by Luis Naranjo.

El Altar needs no translation into English and its various peaks all bear church related names. The highest is El Obispo (the bishop), 5319 m, but its height is much in dispute, with some authorities suggesting as much as 5465 m. This was the first peak to be climbed. The Italians, led by Tremonti, played an important part in the conquest of El Altar's peaks. They returned in 1965 to conquer the second peak, El Canonigo (the canon), 5260 m, and in 1972 achieved the first ascent of El Fraile Grande (the great friar). The three other Fraile peaks were all climbed for the first time by Ecuadorian teams. Bernado Beate, Jacinto Carrasco, and Rafael Terán were the summit climbers in two of those first ascents. La Monja Grande (the great nun), the third highest peak at 5160 m, was climbed by a US–Japanese team in 1968 and the remaining two peaks, La Monja Chica (the little nun) and El Tabernaculo (the tabernacle) fell to a German team in 1972.

This volcano is obviously not a jaunt for the beginning climber, but a backpacking trip is very rewarding. There is a grey-green crater lake called, curiously, Laguna Amarilla (yellow lake), and from the edge of the crater backpackers can listen to the hanging glaciers crack and rumble and catch glimpses of enormous ice slides. Condors are also seen around here. All in all, a fine mountain experience.

GETTING THERE   From Quito's Terminal Terrestre, take a bus via Ambato to Baños, and continue on to Penipe, about halfway to Riobamba. From Penipe you must make your way to Candelaria, about 15 km away up the Río Blanco valley. It's quite a steep climb.

The most reliable transport along this route is the *lechera*, or milk truck, departing Penipe at about 6 a.m. On Thursday, Saturday and Sunday there is a mid-morning truck. The Penipe market is on Sunday, so all day there are various vehicles bound for Candelaria. There is also a driver who will take you in his pickup truck from Penipe to Candelaria and Hacienda Releche. Ask around the main plaza for Ernesto Haro B. He charges about US $5 and will pick you up for the return trip at a pre-arranged time if you wish.

For the return from Candelaria to Penipe you can catch the *lechera* between 6 and 7 a.m. or ask the teachers for a lift when they leave at about noon.

In Candelaria there is a small store with very basic food supplies and they may be able to suggest somewhere you can sleep. There are also mules available to pack your gear up to the base of the mountain. Return pick up times can be arranged.

HIKING DIRECTIONS

From Candelaria continue along the road, over the Río Choca to a blue house some 2 to 3 km from Candelaria. This is the Hacienda Releche beyond which the trail begins. The trail leads uphill to your left, past a few buildings, and continues to some fields. This is the only confusing part since there are now only cow paths running up

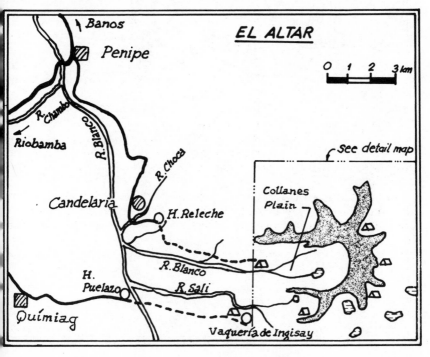

through the meadows. The trail to El Altar goes high on the west-facing hillside just below a waterfall but above the cultivated fields. The trail is just behind the trees and is not visible from below, but if you follow the cowpaths uphill through the fields you will come to it. Once you connect with the main trail turn right and stride out. There are no other paths to confuse you.

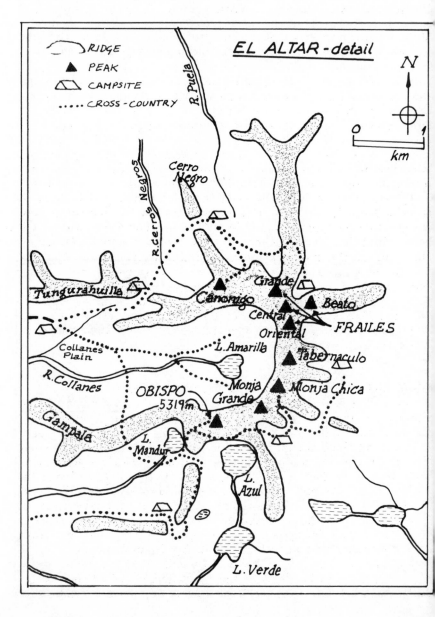

The trail heads east, passing through scrubby woodlands, going gently uphill before rounding a corner and giving you your first views of El Altar and its river valley. A marvellous sight. From there it's a gentle 3 hours of nearly level walking until you arrive at the broad pasture known as Collanes. This is normally as far as the mules will take you (unless you're going northeast towards Canonigo) and it is often used as a campsite. Too often, in fact, judging by the amount of trash I saw there. This section takes 5 to 8 hours from Candelaria. You can cross the Collanes plain to the trees at the base of the crater to camp out of the wind. Edward Whymper did just that in 1880.

From the Collanes plain there are three basic choices, assuming, that is, you wish to do anything at all. You can go east and visit the crater; you can go south to climb the southern peaks (including Obispo, the highest) or do some backpacking in a beautifully wild and trackless area with many lakes; or you can go north to climb the northern peaks (including Canonigo, the second highest) and do some backpacking in this area which is little explored. A challenging and adventurous hike would be all the way around the back of the mountain – there are no maps and it is rarely done.

The best route from Collanes to the rim of the crater is up along the wooded ridge on the left of the river (follow cow paths), heading toward the deeply incised rock face. Although you can go around the hill at the left of the ridge, the shortest route up is the gully just to the right of the knob at the end of the wooded ridge. The first 5 m are very steep, but not difficult as there is tussock grass to hang onto and flat places where you can regain your breath. If it has been raining you might feel safer (and drier) taking the long route around to your left, but you'll have to climb much higher.

For the return trip, consider hiking to Hacienda Puelazo via Vaquería de Ingisay (see below).

CLIMBING OBISPO AND THE SOUTHERN PEAKS

From Collanes head south and climb over the Gampala ridge. (I camped on the ridge for spectacular views of Altar, Tungurahua, Carihuairazo, and Chimborazo.) From Gampala ridge drop to Laguna Mandur and climb the Negra Paccha ridge to a small pass near where the Italian camp was situated. Continue north to the lower glacier and cross it to the base of Obispo. The Italian Route climbs the wide and obvious gully and passes through a rock band to the upper glacier. Traverse the upper glacier to the right until you reach the base of a second snow gully, much steeper and narrower than the first. This gully brings you to the summit ridge. Head right and you'll be faced with a difficult 30 m high rock wall which is the final barrier to the summit. To avoid the first gully, one can climb to the upper glacier on the ridge to the right. This is called the Calvary Ridge route. A bivouac may be necessary. Rappels are usually used for the descent.

An alternative access route is often used instead of the Candelaria–Collanes trail described. From Riobamba get a bus to Quimiag and hitch-hike or walk to the Hacienda Puelazo. Mules can be hired here and you head east on a trail towards the Vaquería de Ingisay, which is a shepherds' hut a day's journey from Puelazo. Camp is usually made before you reach the Vaquería. The next day continue east on cow paths along the Negra Paccha ridge and make a camp on the ridge. The third day is spent following the ridge to the Italian camp. Fit and acclimatized climbers may be able to combine these 2 days into one long one. Although this route is longer, it has the advantage that the mules can get closer to the Italian base camp than Collanes.

To climb the other southern peaks, Monja Grande, Monja Chica, and Tabernaculo, you have to continue from the base of Obispo around the south side of the mountain along the foot of the glacier. Approximate positions for campsites are indicated on the map. Half a dozen major and many minor lakes make this an area of exceptional beauty.

CLIMBING CANONIGO AND THE NORTHERN PEAKS

From the Collanes plain head northeast over the Tungurahuilla ridge where there are possible campsites. Continue to the next ridge, Cerro Negro, where a base camp is made. Mules from Candelaria can reach this point in 2 days – or perhaps one long hard one.

From the base camp on Cerro Negro ridge traverse the glacier which lies to the northeast of Canonigo, the second highest peak of Altar. Head towards the base of a small ridge which leads to a minor eastern summit of Canonigo. Difficult mixed climbing takes you up the western side of this small ridge and you then curve around the crater towards the summit west of you. A bivouac is often necessary. Canonigo is less frequently climbed than Obispo and is more difficult.

To climb the other northern peaks, the four Frailes, continue around the bottom of the northern glaciers to a camp in the cirque of the Frailes. These peaks have had very few ascents.

The only maps of the area available from the IGM are two 1:50,000 planametric maps: P180 and P187. They're not worth buying.

It is rainy most of the year, June and July being the wettest months. The best times to go are from late November through early February, with the majority of successful ascents being made around Christmas and New Year. I have seen one report published in Ecuador which claims that the El Altar region receives 14,600 mm (that's about 48 feet!) of precipitation annually. Although I find this hard to believe, it does at least indicate that the region is wet . . . very wet.

VOLCÁN SANGAY (5230 m)

INTRODUCTION In many ways Sangay is the most difficult and dangerous mountain to climb in Ecuador. It is said to be the most continuously active volcano in South America and the constant shower of red hot rocks and ash make all attempts to climb it an exceedingly hazardous venture. Furthermore it is situated in a very remote region and several days of hard travel are required to reach its base. The volcano is found in the southern central part of the largely inaccessible Sangay National Park, some 200 km south of Quito.

The height of Sangay is usually given as 5230 m but constant activity periodically alters this. The shape of the cone and the number of craters are also constantly changing. The volcanologist Minard L. Hall recorded three main craters and several smaller ones during investigations in 1976.

The first recorded eruption was in 1628 but it was doubtless active before that date. The next 100 years were apparently quiet but since 1728 the volcano has been erupting almost continuously. In 1849 the Frenchman, Sebastián Wisse, explored the area and counted 267 strong explosions within one hour. A short spell of inactivity occurred from 1916 to 1934 and it was during this time that the volcano was first ascended. The U.S. climbers Robert T. and Terris Moore, Paul Austin, and Lewis Thorne reached the summit on August 4, 1929. Attempts since then have claimed the lives of several climbers, including two British mountaineers who died in 1976 as recorded in the book *Sangay Survived* by Richard Snailham. Despite the constant eruptions and danger several successful ascents by Ecuadorian climbers have been reported in the 70s and 80s. On September 16, 1982, Helena Landázuri, of the Fundación Natura, became the first woman to reach the summit. The following account is based on a recent interview I had with Helena in the offices of the Fundación Natura in Quito.

THE APPROACH AND CLIMB The initial stages of the approach are simple: take one of many buses from Quito's Terminal Terrestre to Riobamba. From Riobamba several buses a day go to Licto or Pungala, about 20 km south southeast of Riobamba. From Licto or Pungala occasional trucks go into Alao, which is the starting point for any attempt on Sangay.

Alao is a very small village which nevertheless boasts a few small shops where basic last minute supplies may be purchased. There is also a national park station and two park wardens who will let you sleep in the station for a nominal fee. Normally a permit is required to do this and is obtainable from the Intendente del Parque Nacional Sangay at the MAG offices (Ministerio de Agricultura y Ganaderia) in Riobamba. Phone 61987. Both the MAG office and the park wardens can give you recent information on Sangay's state of activity but don't expect the wardens to accompany you as guides unless you are a scientific expedition and go through the normal bureaucratic channels.

From Alao you have to reach Hacienda Eten. The road to the *hacienda* goes south from the 'main' road just before Alao. A truck can be rented in Alao to get you to the *hacienda*; it takes about 2 hours up the very bad dirt road which may be almost impassable after heavy rains and four wheel drive may be required. At Eten it is advisable to hire mules and this may take several days to arrange. It is

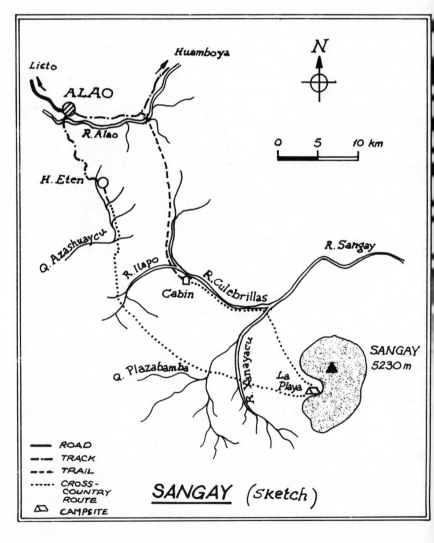

SANGAY (Sketch)

suggested that an advance party goes to Eten to arrange mule hire about a week before your expedition and equipment go in. It is difficult to find guides who know the route; there is no trail and you have to go cross-country.

From Eten to the base of the volcano takes about four days. The first day you head more or less south along the Quebrada Azashuay-cu and camp in an area known as Escaleras, continuing the next day in a roughly southeast direction to Plazabamba. The going is very up and down as you constantly climb rises and cross rivers. In one day fourteen river fordings were reported. The vegetation here is not too thick. Plazabamba is a large flat low area which can be seen from quite a distance. There is a simple shelter which is easy to find in the flat plain. Two long, hard days are needed to get here. (After leaving your first campsite take care not to continue south on rough animal tracks which will lead you to the Tres Cruces area and will waste a lot of time.)

From Plazabamba, there is more vegetation and the terrain becomes increasingly ridged and difficult. There are many streams and small rivers to ford. If a group has been in recently it might be possible to reach the base camp in one very long hard day but normally 2 days of machete work are required. The unevenness of the terrain and thick vegetation cover mean that finding an area for tenting is extremely difficult; you may have to sleep under a tree and a poncho. The base camp is approximately east southeast of Plazabamba. Although you are now close to the mountain, almost constant cloud makes a sighting infrequent.

The base camp is made at about 3600 m in a region known as La Playa on the southwest side of the mountain. Mules cannot get in all the way because of the rough terrain. La Playa is an obvious red lava flow flanked by streams. There is a flattish platform of several hundred square metres in size which is used for the camp. Set up tents as close to the mountain as possible. There are signs of previous camps and a plaque commemorating Adrian Ashby-Smith and Ronald Mace, the two British climbers killed in 1976.

At the base camp you can expect to hear explosions every 5 to 10 minutes but clouds often obscure the volcano during the day making night time viewing the best. You will wake up in the morning to find your tent covered with a layer of ash. Although it is hard work to reach this point you are still not in danger from falling rocks. The ascent to the summit can be done in some 8 hours but changing conditions make it impossible to give a standard route. The party which Srta. Landázuri was with climbed to the right onto the southeastern flanks of the volcano for their ascent and frequent rock showers were heard and seen. The return to the Hacienda Eten from the base camp could be accomplished in 2 very long days.

Other routes have been reported as well. Chris Bonington was there in 1966 and records his experiences in his book *The Last*

Horizon. He climbed up from the southeast via the Río Upano and Río Volcán. It took him 9 days and he wrote, ". . . every foot of the way had to be hacked from the impenetrable entanglement presented by the undergrowth." Doesn't sound like much fun! He also reports his ice axe turning a dull yellow-green because of the sulphurous fumes.

Bonington, Koerner, Snailham and Kelsey all report a different route from Alao, although Helena Landázuri considers this would take longer than the one she described. A very bad four wheel drive road continues east from Alao to a pasture area above which is a stream and waterfalls. A 'trail' heads south from here, zigzagging up and down the mountain to a cabin some 2 days walk away. From here one heads southeast along the Río Culebrillas to the Río Sangay from where one heads roughly south to the La Playa base camp. Doubtless other routes can be used as well.

There are no good maps covering the region. The IGM makes two 1:50,000 planametric maps covering the area but they show little detail apart from the rivers and the position of the volcano. The maps are 194 Sangay and 201 Lago Tinguichaca. Obviously you must bring plenty of food and raingear. Hard hats provide a little protection from rock showers. A rope is not recommended since the ascent is technically very easy and being roped up severely limits your ability to dodge falling rocks. Crampons and ice axe are useful on the summit slopes but not essential. Many groups carry two way radios.

Attempts can and are made year round but December to February are the driest and best months. July and August are the wettest and other months are also very wet.

THE ACHIPUNGO-SOROCHE AREA

This area (sometimes also known as Ayapungo) is a remote and rarely visited region about 230 km south of Quito. It is a lake district which includes Laguna Cubillín, the second largest lake in the Ecuadorian highlands, and many smaller lakes. They are prettily surrounded by mountains, the highest of which usually have some snow on them. These are Cerro Achipungo (4630 m) and Cerro Soroche (4730 m). Reaching the area is time consuming, but once you're there you can enjoy weeks of undisturbed exploration.

Several access routes are possible. One way is to enter the region from the north at the Lagunas de Atillo. To reach these lakes follow directions in the *Andes to Jungle* hike described next. Another route is from Laguna Sansahuín which lies 25 to 30 km to the southeast – this would be a long and adventurous hike. Laguna Sansahuín can be reached from the Inca road to Ingapirca described in Chapter 4. From the starting point of the Inca road, Achupallas, there's a track to Osogochi which is near Laguna Cubillín. Make enquiries in Achupallas. Finally, a dirt road leaves the Pan American Highway about 7 km south of Palmira and heads through Pozorrumi and Totoras towards Osogochi. If you can find the road and have a jeep, this is probably the quickest access.

The IGM publishes a good 1:50,000 topographic map: Totoras. This shows Osogochi, Laguna de Cubillín, Lagunas de Atillo, Cerros Achipungo and Soroche. More maps will be needed for access from other areas. This is an area for experienced campers, hikers, and mountaineers who want to get as far off the beaten track as possible.

FROM THE ANDES TO THE JUNGLE

In the course of a day, the nakedness of the Interior changed to
the luxuriousness of the tropics; ... we passed through forest
trees rising 150 feet high, mast-like, without a branch, laden with
parasitic growth.
Edward Whymper, 1892.

INTRODUCTION Walking through windswept *páramo*, passing
remote thatched huts and bundled up Indians herding sheep, crossing
a high Andean pass, and then dropping down through lush high
mountain forest into the jungles of the Oriente – this is an adventurous hike which shows a remarkable cross section of Ecuador's
scenery, vegetation, and wildlife.

The locals walk this trail in 3 long days, but I recommend twice
this if you are to enjoy the scenery and observe some of the wildlife.

The hike begins in the highlands south of the major town of Riobamba, then crosses a pass in the Eastern Cordillera some 30 km
southwest of the continuously active volcano, Sangay, before dropping steeply into the huge wilderness area of the almost trackless
Sangay National Park. You finally emerge at the small but important
town of Macas, about 1000 m above sea level, situated on the
Río Upano on the edge of Ecuadorian Amazonia.

Macas was first settled by the Spaniards nearly 400 years ago and
the trail follows the old communication and trading route joining the
lowlands with the highlands. Thus the hike is of historical as well as
geographical and ecological interest. Today Macas is at the end of
an unasphalted road running north–south along the banks of the
Upano river. The northbound road to Puyo is still under construction and peters out a few kilometres north of Macas; the southbound
road goes through Sucúa and then on to Cuenca, the nearest major
city, some 12 hours away. So Macas still remains very isolated. A
road is projected westwards over the highlands to Guamote and the
first section to the Río Abanico, some 20 km west of Macas, has
been completed. The rest of the road will more or less follow the old
trail, but lack of funds and difficulty of terrain make it highly unlikely that the road will be completed for many years to come.

WEATHER AND TIMES TO GO In the highland section, you are just
west enough to experience the weather pattern of the central highlands. The typical dry season is from June through September, with
a short dry season in late December and early January and wet other
wise. The lowlands are always wet but the least rainy months are late
September through December. We went during the first week in
October and more or less avoided rain, but it seems as if most other
periods (with the exception of late December) will have rain during
one part of the hike or another.

EQUIPMENT   If you follow my route description carefully you'll find it feasible to get by without a tent – a shelter will be suggested for every night. But a tent is useful for complete independence, so good campsites will also be mentioned. The difficulty, of course, is that the warm clothing needed for the highlands will be unnecessary weight in the lowlands. I partially solved the problem by bringing a very light sleeping bag and sleeping in my clothes in the highlands. Rain gear is essential. I found ex-army jungle boots the best footwear because regular boots soon became hopelessly waterlogged and heavy in the deep mud of the lowland section. I made a point of always keeping a dry shirt, pair of trousers, and sneakers in a plastic bag. This way I always had warm, dry clothes to put on in the evenings, even if I'd spent hours sloshing through calf deep mud and bogs during the day. (This system only works if you're prepared to dress in your wet and muddy hiking outfit every morning.) Insect repellant is useful, although the bugs are not bad. Very little food is available en route and you should bring enough for 5 to 6 days.

MAPS   Five 1:50,000 IGM maps cover the trail. They are (in the order you will use them) the Guamote, Palmira, and Totoras topographical maps (detailed and useful), and the Zuñac 206 and Macas 207 planametric maps which have little detail.

GETTING THERE   Take a bus from Quito's Terminal Terrestre to Riobamba, and make your way to Barrio El Dolorosa (a taxi will take you there cheaply). The next town on your route, Cebadas, is reached by a Cooperativa de Transportes Unidos (CTU) bus which leaves daily at 3 p.m. from the intersection two blocks away from El Dolorosa bus terminal. There is an extra bus on Wednesdays and three additional ones on Saturdays going to Cebadas. Three buses a week continue through Cebadas to Pancun; this is because one of the drivers lives there. You'll have to ask the CTU bus drivers in Riobamba to find out which bus will go on to Pancun. It is also possible to hire a pickup truck to take you the 12 to 15 km from Cebadas to Pancun or, of course, you can walk. There are no proper hotels in Cebadas but if you're persistent you'll find a place to stay. Pancun is just a huddle of a few houses; you can easily camp near here or ask in the main house if you can sleep in a barn. This section can easily be followed on the 1:50,000 Guamote map. (Although a road joins Cebadas with Guamote, it is in very bad condition and has only one regular truck a week driving along it.)
   From Pancun the dirt road continues south (change to the 1:50,000 Palmira map) through El Reten to El Tingo which is some 20 km south of Pancun. The owner of the pickup truck in Pancun will give you a lift for about US $6 or $8 (ask at the main house). There are

also vehicle owners in Cebadas who will drive you to El Tingo. The dirt road roughly follows the Río Cebadas southwards to El Tingo; it is fairly flat and campsites aren't difficult to find if you want to walk. We began the hike from El Tingo which is the end of the road. There are a few houses here and people will give you shelter if you ask.

EL TINGO TO MACAS – HIKING DIRECTIONS

A suitable distance for the first hiking day is from El Tingo to Atillo. This is an extremely pleasant and not difficult 5 to 7 hour walk through gently rising pastureland with starkly beautiful rather than spectacular views. You'll see herds of sheep, cattle, and perhaps semi-wild horses. The people are politely friendly but rather reserved and obviously not used to backpackers. The vegetation is grassy. You are within sight of the river all the way and there is plenty of water.

Just beyond the end of the dirt road the track crosses a footbridge over the Río El Tingo and continues as a well defined footpath along the east side of Río Cebadas. After about 2 km the river makes a Y and here you follow the trail along the left-hand bank of the left hand fork (Río Yasipán) for about a kilometre until you come to a bridge which you cross. The trail climbs over a small hill and then drops back to the Río Cebadas which it follows for over a kilometre until the river divides into two: the Río Osogochi to the right and the Río Atillo to the left. The trail also forks and you take the left hand one along the east side of the Río Atillo. In a couple of kilometres the trail goes through the straggling community of Colay (a few houses and a schoolhouse) and continues south and southeast through the wide river valley to the village of Atillo some 7 to 8 km beyond Colay. En route you will change from the Palmira to the Totoras map. Atillo is distinguished by a church, a cemetery, and a schoolhouse in which you can sleep. There are plenty of good campspots in the area before Atillo, or you can continue for about an hour beyond the village to campsites with perhaps better views.

If you've been following the 1:50,000 IGM maps you'll find the trail is quite accurately marked until here, but don't be misled into taking the left fork at Atillo. The route goes along the right fork around the hillock marked 3526 m on the map. This track soon curves around to the east and heads along the northern shores of the Laguna de Atillo. There are good campsites here with fine views of the lakes and the occasional snowpeaks of Cerros Achipungo (4630 m), Yanaurco, and Sasquín beyond the lakes to the south. Don't camp too close to the lakes as the banks are boggy; it's best to camp on the hillocks just north of the first lake. There are streams for drinking water.

The second day is in many ways the most spectacular of the whole hike as you cross a pass in the Eastern Cordillera and start dropping down into the Amazonian rain forest. The change in vegetation is remarkable. Standing on the pass, you see the stark grassy *páramo* stretching away behind you, while in front huge cloud masses build up from the lowlands as the highlands fall away into incredibly lush cloud forest full of bromeliads and birdsong. Stands of huge trees rear out of the dense carpet of lower foliage and everywhere you look is covered with seemingly impenetrable vegetation. The change from bleak *páramo* to tropical cloud forest is so sudden it stuns your credibility – it has to be seen to be believed.

The trail is quite easily followed on the north sides of the Lagunas de Atillo and then forks by the third lake, Laguna Cuyo. The two trails meet again high on a ridge beyond this lake so you can take your choice. The higher trail may be less muddy if it has been wet. The trail continues through mud around the northern shore of Laguna Negra and reaches the crest of the *cordillera* some 2 to 3 hours from the camp by the Lagunas de Atillo. By now you are passing through a tunnel of thick vegetation but there are occasional gaps in the green walls for you to admire the spectacular views. Here you change to your 1:50,000 planametric map of Zuñac.

At this point you'll have to accept that you're going to get very muddy, say "To hell with it!", and start sloshing on. The steep trail down through the jungle is unmistakable and there are no forks where you could get lost, but it is sometimes used by pack-animals and is usually churned up with thick mud. Occasional slippery logs are a psychological aid, although when you slide off them and end up in the muck you may not feel that they are all that helpful!

After an hour of very steep descent the trail flattens out and follows the south side of the deeply cut Río Upano valley. About 2 to 3 hours beyond the divide you'll cross a small stream (with possible but stony campspots on either side). It's better to continue for nearly an hour to a small thatched shelter on the right of the trail. The stream just mentioned is your best water source, but there are also smaller trickles every few hundred metres. You can spend the night camping on a small, flat, grassy area in front of the hut or sleep in the dirt-floored shelter. There is a good view across the river valley from this spot.

The following day will be an extremely muddy one. Sloshing along the trail isn't really much fun; what we did was make this a half day's walk and then spend the afternoon at the next campsite which boasts good views and the chance to admire the flowers, trees, bromeliads, and thick vegetation and to observe colourful insects and various bird species such as hummingbirds and parrots. Why rush? Relax and enjoy your unusual surroundings – easier to do from a dry camp than along the trail.

From the first hut continue about two hours to a second one. This has a tin roof and wooden floor. Continue about 2 more hours to the third hut which is suitable for passing the afternoon and spending the night. You can't get lost on the trail. Near the third hut is a Sangay National Park sign.

The fourth day will see you continuing eastwards following the slowly dropping Río Upano valley through lush vegetation and ending up at an unusual campsite. . . . From the third hut, about three hours of hiking will bring you to the settlement of Purshi which is marked on the map with ten hopeful looking squares. In fact I could find only one locked building and a totally useless and decrepit hut – there are a few grass huts high up on the other side of the river with no visible trail or bridge. You could camp here if you wanted, though there are some rather wild looking cattle which would probably love to rub themselves up against your tent, but about 1½ hours beyond Purshi you come to a covered bridge crossing the Río Playas. This bridge, some 10 m long and 2 m wide and with a tin roof, provided us with a unique campsite where we were lulled to sleep by the rushing rapids below. Be careful not to drop anything though; you certainly wouldn't see it again.

If you don't like the idea of sleeping on the bridge then you could continue for about an hour to the village marked as Zuñac on the map but known locally as Playas after the nearby river. The village consists of about two dozen buildings scattered around a large grass square, and there is a church and a schoolhouse where you could probably sleep. This is the first settlement after Atillo. Although the distance from Atillo to Zuñac looks relatively short on the map, the extremely winding trail makes it a much longer hike than the map indicates.

On the fifth day you will be walking through more cultivated countryside with plenty of signs of settlement. You'll probably meet a few people driving mules up the trail, or a woodcutter or smallholder. They'll usually stop for a chat and are good sources of information about the trail ahead. The trail beyond Zuñac is blessedly firmer and less muddy. From Zuñac 1½ hours of steep climbing will bring you to two or three huts marking the community of San Vicente. A couple of hours beyond San Vicente the bridge marked on the planametric map has been washed out. Unless it's been rebuilt you'll have to cross the Río San Francisco about 100 m downstream over a crude log bridge and follow a steep new trail up the opposite bank to meet with the old trail. About an hour further you pass through San Francisco which is also only two or three houses. Some 2 hours more bring you to Nueve de Octubre which is the largest community on the hike but unmarked on the maps. You could spend the night in a school house here.

A dirt road is being built from Macas to Nueve de Octubre which is the end of the cross-cordillera road planned from Guamote to Macas. At the time of writing the roadhead has reached a point about an hour beyond Nueve de Octubre. From the roadhead we walked about 5 km through bulldozed mud with remarkable suction properties before reaching the road proper. The last 20 km to Macas can be covered by hitching a ride on the workers' truck. They finish work about 2 pm on weekdays.

Macas is a gateway town into the jungle. Views of the nearby active volcano Sangay are good on clear days (rare) and it is a useful centre for day hikes into the surrounding countryside (see *The Macas Area* in Chapter 7). There are several cheap and basic hotels and plenty of restaurants. You're back in the twentieth century.

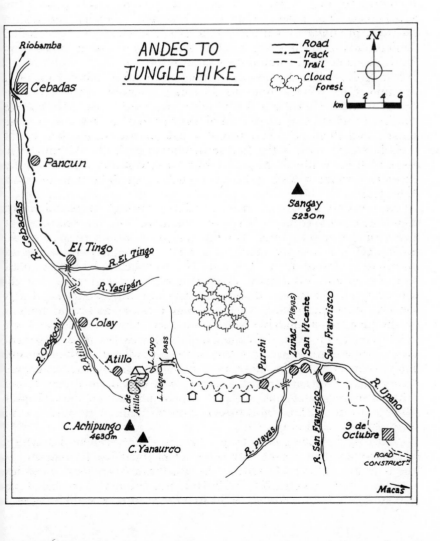

CHAPTER 7
THE ORIENTE

INTRODUCTION

The Oriente is the name given to Ecuador's Amazonia, a huge lowland area east of the Andes and comprising 36% of Ecuador's total territory. Popularly known as 'the jungle', the region is properly referred to as 'tropical rain forest'. Dense, hot, and wet, just as one would expect it to be, the Oriente was largely unexplored and untravelled until the oil boom of the 1960s. Now four dirt roads penetrate the region and access is relatively straightforward.

Without a doubt, the most fascinating aspect of the Oriente is its incredible variety of flora and fauna. This is partly due to the so-called edge effect. This means that any region where two different ecological zones are in sharp juxtaposition will have a greater variety of species than a region where two ecological zones gradually merge. The dramatic drop of the Andes to the Oriente is sudden enough to produce this effect. Over 700, or half, of Ecuador's bird species have been recorded in the Oriente; this is roughly equivalent to all the species found in the United States. About 3000 species of butterfly are known in Ecuador; this represents an incredible 15% of the world's butterflies. Sloths, armadillos, and anteaters are present members of the strange Edentate family which is found only in Neotropica. On a single 10 day trip into the Oriente (admittedly to a remote region) I saw six different species of monkey. And, of course there are countless insects, many of which still prove to be new to science when classified. The trees and plants are no less varied and interesting; the giant buttressed ceibal tree, the chonta palm covered with thousands of needle sharp thorns over its trunk, and the blossoms muskily scenting the forest all contribute to this fascinating natural wilderness.

Ecuador, land of volcanoes, even manages to produce a couple of volcanoes perched on the very edge of the lowlands. Rearing out of the rain forest, they are the active Reventador (3485 m) and the presently dormant Sumaco (3900 m). Both mountains have slopes dropping within 25 km to high Amazonian forests at 1200 m.

Although roads now penetrate the lowlands, and airstrips occasionally puncture the rain forest, some of the most satisfying journeys into the jungle will be by dugout canoe and on foot. This section describes a variety of trips to different areas with an emphasis on hiking and dugouts.

THE MISAHUALLÍ AREA

For the traveller with a limited amount of time, a trip to the small river port of Misahuallí on the Río Napo will give a good glimpse of the Oriente.

The journey begins at Baños, the prettily situated gateway town to the Oriente (see *The Baños Area* in Chapter 6). From here you take a bus to Puyo which is the capital of the lowland province of Pastaza. Only 66 km away from Baños, it lies just 950 m above sea level. The winding gravel road follows the Pastaza river valley and, as it drops, you can appreciate the rapidly changing vegetation and the many waterfalls (one of which cascades from an overhanging cliff onto the road - a damp experience in a pick-up truck). From the narrow confines of the Río Pastaza gorge, the first sudden sighting of the Amazonian plains is breathtaking. There is an obligatory passport control in Shell-Mera, some 15 km before Puyo.

From Puyo, if the weather is clear, you can view various snow-capped peaks rising over 4000 m above you and only 50 km distant. Sangay is sometimes visible, exploding away some 65 km to the southwest. Several buses a day leave Puyo for Tena. Get off the bus at Puerto Napo, some 75 km beyond Puyo and 7 km before Tena. From Puerto Napo, frequent pick-up trucks act as a bus service to Puerto Misahuallí, at the end of the road 17 km away.

Now you're in the tropical lowlands, just 600 m above sea level. It's amazing to realize that only 80 km away to the northwest Antisana towers over 5000 m above you, whilst the mouth of the Amazon at Belém lies over 3000 km to the east, with no higher ground in between.

Just 15 years ago Puerto Misahuallí was no more than a huddle of a few huts, but the oil boom, the new road, and tourism have enlarged it to several hundred inhabitants. It is still a very sleepy little port, with only very basic hotels and restaurants. The main event is the Sunday river market, when gaily painted dugout canoes powered by modern outboard motors arrive at Misahuallí's sandy beach loaded down with cargoes varying from bananas to parrots. It is an exciting hubbub, with gold panners selling their few grams of precious dust to the city middlemen, hardy colonists trying to sell their corn, bananas, papayas and other produce, pretty Indian girls being eyed by the young men of the local military post, and the occasional Auca Indian, with distended ear lobes, going about the difficult business of integrating into twentieth century life.

Just a generation ago, the region east of here was the territory of the Indians known as the Aucas, which in Quechua means 'savage'. In 1956 five missionaries were killed by the Aucas. Oil was discovered at about this time and the now important town of Coca founded. Killings by both settlers and Indians continued into the 60s but by the 70s the situation had stabilized with the Aucas withdrawing to remote regions of the jungle, as they have done for centuries to avoid genocidal conflicts. In 1983 a reservation of 66,570 hectares was set aside for them in a remote region where, for the time being, they are able to continue life in a relatively traditional manner. Nevertheless, some Aucas are now undergoing the painful change from their simple livelihoods to a twentieth century society – a process which is so rapid that it proves very traumatic and often fatal to many primitive peoples.

Some 2 to 3 days' walk away from Misahuallí is an Auca Indian village. As often as twice a week local guides take groups of tourists there to gawk. The Indians sit around miserably with little interest in their surroundings or the visitors who have come to see them. Seeing the parade of goods which to us seem basic: shoes, backpacks, sunglasses, cameras, penknives, matches, etc., is a disorientating experience for these people. For the visitors, it is sad to visit a group of bewildered looking Indians who are losing their traditional values and abilities. What promised to be an exciting adventure to see 'real' primitive Indians turns out to be a long, uncomfortable trek with a somewhat shaming conclusion.

If you want to see the Indians – wait until they come to you. A few of the more adventurous and acculturated Aucas usually come to the Sunday market in Misahuallí and you can see them and they can see you in an unstrained and uncompromising atmosphere.

Even if you don't normally take organized tours, I feel that some of those offered in Misahuallí are both inexpensive and worthwhile. Several outfitters organize tours; two good ones are Douglas Clarke (Ecuadorian despite his name), and Héctor Fialles of Fluvial River Tours. Tours range from one day walks in the nearby jungles to 10 day trips reaching close to the Peruvian border. Usually a minimum of 5 people are needed (more for longer trips) but there are plenty of gringos in Misahuallí looking for companions. Food, transportation, and accommodation are provided for US $6 to $15 a day depending on the difficulty and duration of the trip. It must be remembered that the immediate area has been colonized so you won't see much in the way of monkeys, wild pigs and so on. Local wildlife is limited to birds and insects which are varied and colourful. A trip along the river near Misahuallí often produces sightings of egrets, vultures, wild turkeys, toucans, anis, tanagers, caciques, and oropendulas. A recommended one day walk into the jungle is Douglas Clarke's waterfall trip. Keep your eyes open for well-camouflaged stick insects, fist sized toads, armies of ants, and hosts of colourful butterflies. Ask to be shown the Achiote (*Bixa orellana*), a plant which is crushed to produce a red paint for body decorations, and a vine containing water fit to drink. A good guide will be able to show you much you would have missed on your own, particularly if you ask many questions and convey your interest and enthusiasm.

If you can get a group together and take a longer tour you will see more wildlife. These tours are not for the soft traveller, but you'll certainly see monkeys, caymans, macaws, and parrots, and with any luck pacas, capybaras, anteaters, armadillos, wild pigs, and . . . who knows, a tapir or a jaguar?

CONTINUING INTO THE ORIENTE

From Misahuallí, you can continue downriver by daily dugout (11.30 a.m.) for the 6 hour journey to the town of Coca. The Río Napo has long been travelled and settled, so don't expect to see monkeys and wild Indians, but you will see dramatic views of the forest and many birds including parrots. Coca is a ramshackle town with little to recommend it; trips further downriver are irregular and expensive since the closing of the mission station at Limoncocha and the restriction on crossing the frontier into Peru at Nuevo Rocafuerte.

From Coca daily buses head north to Lago Agrio, another jungle town produced by the oil boom. It is the most eastern town of any size in Ecuador. The Sunday market brings in members of the local Cofan tribe, with the men often wearing their typical *kushma*, or knee length smock, and perhaps a headband of porcupine quills around their short hair. They often bring necklaces of feathers, seeds, teeth, and even insect wings to sell to tourists.

From Lago Agrio a dirt road follows the oil line to Quito, some 265 km and 10 hours away by bus. The road passes the active volcano Reventador (3485 m) and the village of Baeza, both described later in this chapter, and continues past Volcán Antisana (5704 m) and the village of Papallacta (see Chapter 6) before reaching Quito.

A less time consuming return from Puerto Misahuallí to Quito is by bus via Tena (several a day from Misahuallí). Tena is the capital of Napo province. Good views are often had of the dormant volcano Sumaco (3900 m) about 50 km north northeast. From Tena buses continue on the new dirt road north which runs parallel to the Andes, passing through Archidona and on to Baeza nearly 100 km away. Archidona is famous as being the centre from which you can visit the large cave complex of Jumandi. Unfortunately, the stalactite hunter and phantom spray painter have reached the caves before you, and they are now a rather sorry sight.

A final note about the weather. It can rain year round but June through August seem to be the wettest around Misahuallí. November and December have the least rain. During these times the Río Napo could be either too high or too low to make a boat trip.

"We came again
into the Land of the
Butterflies, and saw the great
Morphos sailing to and fro,
with myriads of attendant
satellites in chrome,
carmine and vermilion".
Whymper

REVENTADOR (3485 m)

INTRODUCTION   Reventador lies 90 km east northeast of Quito. Its name means exploder and this volcano has been frequently active as far back as records go - the first recorded eruption was in 1541. For many years little was known about the area and it was not until 1931 that an Ecuadorian, L. Paz y Miño, visited the area to study it and map it for the first time. It remained relatively inaccessible until the building of the trans-Ecuadorian oil pipeline began in the late 1960s. This in turn prompted the construction of a road from Baeza to the new oil boom town of Lago Agrio and it is from this new road that access to Reventador is made.

Reventador consists of a large outer crater some 2 to 3 km across within which is a huge volcanic cone hundreds of metres high. Extrapolating from the outer crater one can assume that it must once have been one of the highest mountains in the country.

During the mid 1970s Reventador was in a highly active phase and its eruptions are said to have equalled those of the famous Sangay. Major activity ceased in the late 70s and today Reventador merely emits fairly continuous but gentle puffs of steam and gases. This situation could change dramatically thus rendering my route description inaccurate. Check with locals before you climb.

MAPS   No large scale topographical maps are available. The IGM produces a 1:50,000 planametric map (sheet 81) which is only moderately useful. If you follow my description carefully you won't need a map beyond the sketch map provided.

WEATHER AND TIMES TO GO   A friend who lives in the Lago Agrio area claims to have driven the Lago Agrio–Quito road dozens of times but has only seen Reventador twice, although it is only 12 km from the road as the crow flies. The area is very wet and usually cloudy. The wettest months are June and July, and the best are September through December - but you can still expect daily showers.

EQUIPMENT   A trail of sorts has been hacked out of the forest so a machete is no longer necessary although it can be helpful as the trail is overgrown. During the 'dry' season, insects aren't a major problem but repellent should be brought during the wetter months. A waterproof tent is a must. My preferred clothing is rain gear (Gore-Tex) over tee shirt and shorts, with a dry shirt and pair of trousers kept in plastic bags for camp and tent wear. It's too warm for a heavy sleeping bag; a blanket and dry clothes are fine to sleep in. The trail is extremely muddy and at times you'll be on hands and knees crawling under trees in 3 inches of mud. My favourite footwear is army style jungle boots; sneakers are just acceptable, but hiking boots become heavy and waterlogged very quickly. A spare pair of sneakers for camp and tent wear mean your feet can dry out occasionally. A large selection of plastic bags is a must. Bring extra water bottles because the last camp is waterless.

GETTING THERE   Catch a bus from Quito's Terminal Terrestre through Baeza to Lago Agrio. Although you will be going only two thirds of the way to Lago Agrio you may be charged the full fare at the bus station. The bus journey is very interesting and worth a description.

The road descends from Quito through several small villages and is paved for about 30 km. At Pifo it changes to dirt and begins the ascent over one of the highest road passes in Ecuador, crossing the Eastern Cordillera at an altitude of nearly 4100 m some 50 km out of Quito. The road then drops to the lake of Papallacta from where an entry may be made to climb Antisana (see Chapter 6). Just before the village of Papallacta, over 60 km from Quito, is a turn off to the left with a sign for thermal baths which are some of the best in the country. The road continues to drop through enchantingly beautiful high mountain forest, with many strange plants and colourful birds. Some 100 km from Quito the road forks; we follow the left fork and proceed through the villages of Borja and El Chaco, from where you may get your first views of Reventador. There are frequent views of the Río Quijos on your right. About 150 km from Quito you cross the Río Azuela on a large steel bridge – this is a major landmark. Some 10 km further a small bridge crosses the Río Malo (the starting point for the 'wrong way' approach). 170 km from Quito you pass a little cement block hut with an INECEL sign at a turnoff to your right. This is where you get off the bus to climb Reventador.

CLIMBING REVENTADOR – THE WRONG WAY

Before giving the directions for this not too difficult climb, let me describe our experiences as pathfinders.

Relatively little information about this volcano was available in Quito – I couldn't find anyone who claimed to have climbed it, and written descriptions were uninviting: "There are reported to be snakes, nasty insects, and 7 metres of rain a year" (Koerner), and "Reventador is still active and potential heroes armed with machetes can try hacking their way through the thick forests which cover its slopes to reach the crater." (*South American Handbook*).

I must admit to certain feelings of trepidation as our little group of three pulled out of the bus terminal in Quito. We had read one route description which told us to go between the two branches of the Río Malo and climb to the rim of the outer crater. From here we could circle clockwise around the rim to the back of the mountain and descend into the crater to make an ascent of the inner cone.

Accordingly, we told the rather surprised bus driver to let us off at the Río Malo bridge, and we were left standing in the middle of nowhere looking rather disconsolately at our three packs and the trackless jungle around us. We couldn't even see the volcano we had come to climb. There was about an hour of daylight left and no obvious camping places so, remembering a small cluster of houses some 2 km back, I suggested we return there, find the inevitable store/bar, and talk to the locals.

After several beers we felt decidedly better adjusted to jungle life and persuaded the landlady to let us have some water (not exactly a rare commodity around here) and camp in front of the store/bar by the pipeline running along the road. The few people around obviously thought we were insane to be going into that thick jungle to look for an active volcano. One person had volunteered the information that he had been about 500 m back from the road – he seemed to think that was quite far enough. So much for our hopes of obtaining information or hiring a guide.

The following morning we left early and walked back to the Río Malo. On the left hand side of the river we could see a thin path leading off into the jungle, so I dropped my pack and trotted along to investigate. It ran close to the river and was easy to follow for several hundred metres so I trotted back to the group and reported it was worth a try.

About a kilometre from the road the path began to peter out and we started to use the machete. If you've never used a machete before you'll find it's harder than it looks. Try to cut branches at an angle rather than through at 90°. And be careful that the machete doesn't fly out of your muddy and sweaty hands with a particularly energetic swing – I nearly decapitated one of my companions this way. When all signs of the path faded we hacked our way to the Río Malo to try walking up the river, which at this point was knee deep. After several hundred metres of wading we came upon an extraordinarily impressive sight: in front of us was a cirque of cliffs some 50 m high with the river cascading down in a spectacular waterfall. So much for our ideas of wading upstream! We were totally unprepared for these falls but decided to continue upstream right to their base; a rather damp but exciting experience.

Our next move was to consider the best way over the cliffs before us. We thought there was a way up to the right some 300 m before the falls and spent most of that afternoon cutting our way up a steep and muddy slope, holding on with one hand to loose and slippery roots whilst swinging the machete with the other hand. Several hours of hard work almost brought us to the top of the slope, at which point we discovered a 7 m high vertical mud cliff. It looked virtually impossible to climb up the crumbling clay, and the cliff extended a long distance either way. This was obviously not the way to go. It was getting late, so in 15 minutes we stumbled and slid our way back down on the trail we had spent laborious hours cutting and set up a camp on a sandbar by the river.

WARNING. Setting up camp close to an unknown jungle river is a risky exercise. Sudden rainstorms high in jungle areas sometimes produce flash-floods, with rivers rising metres in minutes and sweeping away everything in their paths. Our decision to camp on the sand bar was influenced by the fact that the river appeared short on the map and therefore seemed unlikely to flood. Also heavy rains the previous night had not significantly affected the river's height.

The following day we went back to the road which took us less than 2 hours. Although this route is not recommended as an access to Reventador, the trip to the waterfall makes a good day hike. Once back on the road we headed northeast. In about a kilometre we came to a small bridge which we assumed crossed the second branch of the Río Malo, but nowhere between the two branches were we able to find any sign of a trail leading toward Reventador. 10 km of walking brought us to the little cement block INECEL hut on the right hand side. From here a jeep track leads some 2½ km down to a small flat area which has great views of the San Rafael Falls (also known as the Río Coca Falls) and is suitable for camping. The falls are between 145 m and 200 m in height (depending on your reference source). A trail leads from the camping area to close to the bottom of the falls; allow about an hour for the round trip. There is water available from a small waterfall by the jeep trail some 500 m before the camping area. The falls are probably the highest and certainly the most impressive I've seen in Ecuador and well worth the visit. Koerner tells of the discovery of earthworms glowing blue under the bark of trees near the falls. I didn't see any but I did find some twigs and grasses with a blue luminescent fungus growing on them. There's no telling what gringos spending a quiet night by the falls will discover next! Certainly the area is extremely rich in bird and insect life.

Walking back up to the road and turning right, you come to the tiny community of Río Reventador. Ignoring the first few houses you'll see a store on the right side with a sign 'Se Vende Gasolina'. Here you can buy stove fuel, as well as beer and noodles – delicious volcano climbing fare. This is the beginning of your route up Reventador.

CLIMBING REVENTADOR — THE RIGHT WAY

Ask the lady who runs the store to introduce you to one of her two elder sons, Don Jorge or Don Segundo. Jorge has been all the way to the top of the volcano and could guide you there, whilst Segundo only knows the first section to the beginning of the climbers' trail. To get to the beginning of the trail takes about an hour and once there you should have no difficulty in following the trail as described in my account. The first hour to the trail-head is rather complicated however, so it would be worth hiring Jorge or Segundo to show you

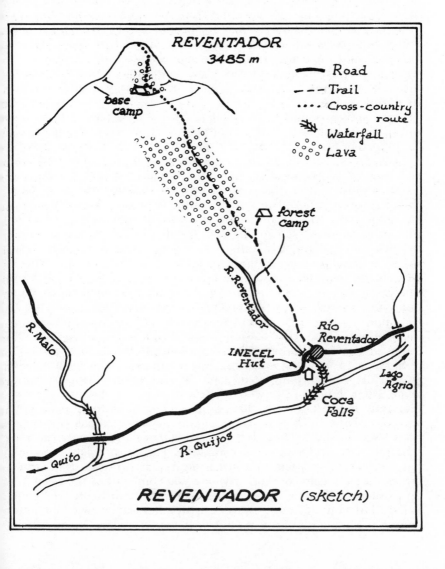

REVENTADOR (sketch)

this section – I paid Segundo 50 sucres for his time.

If neither Jorge nor Segundo is available and you want a guide to the top then you can hire Sr. Guillermo Vasquez who lives in the Pampas area some 4 km closer to Quito. His house is near the school and he is experienced – but by all accounts expensive.

If you are determined to go all the way by yourself then this description might help – but I can't guarantee it! From the store continue climbing up the road till you reach the pipeline. Follow the pipeline until the bottom of the last long steep section disappearing over the skyline. Near here find a faint trail to your left which becomes more visible and crosses fields and lightly wooded areas before reaching a narrow but very slippery stream. After fording this you continue climbing and then go through a gate in a barbed wire fence. Soon you will reach a logged area which you have to cross and then find the trail on the other side. The lack of a well-defined trail and the changing landscape (due to logging) make this section difficult to follow and, again, I recommend hiring a guide for this first hour.

Once at the beginning of the trail you should have no problem following it; it is not for the faint-hearted however, and you should be prepared for a very slippery, muddy, and at times steep hike. Follow the up and down trail for some 2 hours from the trail-head and you will come to a left junction. Straight ahead will bring you (in some 300 m) to a flat area suitable for two or three tents. I call this the forest camp. The nearest water is about 15 minutes back along the trail. *The stream is also the last major supply of water on the whole climb so you should fill up here.* The left fork goes into a recently formed lava field and a trail has been cut through the very thick scrubby new vegetation growing on the lava. This is an extremely difficult section, as the cooling action of the lava has left bubbles and holes big enough to put your leg through. Often these holes are covered with a thin layer of vegetation which is not enough to support your weight – and down you go. As Myles, one of my companions, remarked, "I don't know what's worse, the actual falling in or wondering what evil creatures lurk in those gloomy holes!"

Some 3 to 4 hours will bring you to the end of this lava field. Just before you leave this area, you'll find a tiny ooze which provides some water, but don't rely completely on this. The end of this lower lava flow is marked by a change in vegetation, and you push your way out of the thick scrub onto a higher lava flow which consists of loose and ill-balanced boulders covered with a slippery moss – a combination not conducive to easy walking. This most recent lava field has no discernible track, you just head straight up towards the outer crater. Leave a cairn or marker where you come out of the vegetated area otherwise finding the return trail may prove difficult. The going is hard but you are soon rewarded with a fantastic view of the inner cone rising hundreds of metres out of the outer crater. Directly down the front of the cone are two roughly parallel lava flows and you head approximately northwest to the bottom of the right hand flow. This will bring you to flat areas suitable for camping; allow about 3 hours of rough going from the end of the vegetated area. There is no water. From the road to the crater camp is about 8 hours.

The climb to the summit is a relatively straightforward scramble heading along the right hand of the two lava flows. It will take about 3 hours to reach the summit where you'll find a smoking inner crater, hot sulphur-encrusted rocks, and steam vents. The view of the surrounding jungle is terrific. You can climb up from the crater camp and return to the road in one long day, or you could return to the campsite in the forest. It would be possible to climb from the forest campsite, through the two lava flows, up the inner cone to the summit and back again in one very long day – a dawn start would be essential and you should carry a torch in case you can't get back again within 12 hours.

VOLCÁN SUMACO (3900 m)

This volcano, lying deep in the jungle some 100 km east southeast of Quito, has been known to Europeans since the Spanish conquest when Francisco de Orellana recorded its presence in 1541 after he saw it from the Río Napo during the first stages of his historic first descent of the Amazon. However, its isolated, forest-bound position and generally wet weather have made it one of Ecuador's least known volcanoes.

Although some sources consider Sumaco to be extinct, the few records we have of it indicate that it is an active volcano. Jiménez de la Espada, who made the first ascent in 1865, found a gullied, 100 m wide crater blown open to the south. In 1925, the British climber George M. Dyott climbed Sumaco and recorded that the crater was 270 m wide with no signs of cracks or gullies. This indicates that an eruption must have occurred between the years 1865 and 1925, but the volcano's isolated position prevented this phenomenon from being recorded by any observer. This theory is supported by the fact that Sumaco has a conical shape which, in an environment promoting severe erosion, indicates that activity must have occurred within the last few hundred years. At present there appears to be no activity whatsoever but volcanologists still consider Sumaco to be potentially active.

The volcano has recently become more accessible with the construction of the new Tena–Baeza road, from which another road is planned through Loreto to Coca. When this is finished access will be better. The first few kilometres are still under construction, so don't be too encouraged by new maps of Ecuador which optimistically mark this road as finished. I suppose access must be possible from the Baeza–Lago Agrio road but I haven't met anyone who has been in that way.

After spending a year in Ecuador I had not managed to find any information on how to reach the volcano apart from Koerner's typically laconic "Hire guides and chop east through the jungle for about eight days." My first view of the volcano was from Tena, from the balcony of some Peace Corps volunteers' house. Without any real expectations of hard information, I asked if they had any ideas on how to get up there. "Yeah," they replied, "We climbed it last week." This is what they told me.

Drive up the new Tena–Baeza road to a point 14 km north of Archidona. This is where construction begins for the new road to Coca. Walk about 3 km down the new road and find a trail on your right hand side heading for the village of Huamani. Finding the trail is the most difficult part of the whole trip as construction for the new road has obliterated the junction with the trail. You'll just have to keep looking and asking the occasional person you meet.

Once you're well onto the trail it's difficult to get lost. About an hour from the road you reach a river which must be forded. The trail is muddy with plenty of ups and downs, and the climate hot and humid. Eventually you reach the Río Hollín which is a large river crossed by a bridge. There are areas to camp on the other side. This is almost the halfway point from the road to Huamani. The trail continues clearly to the village and takes one very long hard day from the road. It is better to camp at the Río Hollín and make it two easy days.

Once you get to Huamani you'll find the usual huddle of thatched or tin roofed wooden houses. You will be allowed to sleep in the 'village hall' but don't count on buying food; often there isn't much for sale. The trail ends here and so you should hire a guide. Don Francisco is the main to contact. He will charge US $5-$7 per day. He doesn't have camping equipment so providing him with tent space or at least a large plastic poncho is appreciated. He often brings a friend with him and they hunt monkeys and wild turkeys for food. Bring plenty of your own food if you don't fancy monkey stew, and bring enough for your guides if you want to try to prevent them shooting animals. The men work very hard clearing campsites and starting campfires. About 3 to 5 days are needed for the ascent from Huamani depending on how recently the previous group has been in; the descent along the newly cut trail should take only 2 days. The mountain is thickly vegetated nearly to the summit.

THE BAEZA AREA

Baeza is a small but historical town in the eastern foothills at 1400 m. It was on an ancient trade route even before the conquest. The coming of the Spaniards elevated it to the position of a mission settlement but nowadays no vestiges remain of its past. It is a very quiet place with one basic hotel and a couple of cheap restaurants. It is surrounded by steep hills which could provide days of hiking and exploration. I describe one day hike.

Buses pass through Baeza several times a day on the way to and from Tena. If you are on the Quito–Lago Agrio route you have to walk about 1½ km up the road from the Baeza turnoff. Baeza is about 100 km by road from Quito.

Leave the town plaza on the road going uphill to the right of the church. In a few minutes you will pass the hospital to your left and the cemetery to your right. The trail becomes a stony path. After 15 minutes the trail forks at a foot-bridge. You can go left over the bridge up a steep trail which peters out in fields after about an hour with nice views of Baeza in the valley below. Or you can head straight up the trail (don't cross the river) which takes you through beautiful low mountain pastureland surrounded by trees laden with epiphytes. The birdlife is prolific. I saw hawks and hummingbirds, wrens and woodpeckers, tanagers and thrushes, so bring your binoculars. About 10 minutes past the bridge the trail forks again. Take the right one uphill leaving the stream to your left. A further 10 minutes brings you to a flattish area showing signs of logging. From here the trail becomes increasingly muddy, although stony sections offer relief from the squelch. The trail follows the fence line and then steeply zig-zags over and around a hill. About an hour beyond the logged area it is crossed by a fence and stops suddenly in high pasture on top of a hill. This is a good place for a rest and picnic.

I have prepared a supplementary section on the Galapagos Islands. I you would like a copy please send £1 or $US2 plus a stamped addressed envelope to Bradt Enterprises.

THE MACAS AREA

Though a small town, Macas is the capital of one of the largest provinces in Ecuador, Morona-Santiago. Its history goes back at least four centuries; it was an important Spanish missionary and trading settlement linked with the highlands by a trail still in existence and described in Chapter 6, *From the Andes to the Jungle.*

Despite its provincial capital status, Macas remains a very isolated town. Its airport is being repaired and so the nearest airstrip is Sucúa, 25 km to the south. The road north linking Macas to Puyo is still in the process of construction and will probably be incomplete for several more years. Its main link with the rest of Ecuador is the south-bound road through Sucúa to Cuenca, some 10 hours away by bus.

The Oriente east of Macas is perhaps the least explored region in the entire country. It is the home of the Jívaro Indians, famous for their expertise (now rarely practised) at shrinking the heads of their enemies. Today the Jívaros prefer to call themselves Shuar and are integrating quite rapidly into Ecuadorian society. There is a major Shuar centre in Sucúa which is partially run by Indians and plays an important part in both recording and encouraging traditional life styles as well as aiding the Shuar people in the difficult process of entering twentieth century life, which they seem to be doing with more success than many groups. Nevertheless, some semi-wild groups still exist deep in the forests.

From Macas, trails are marked on the maps which penetrate deeply into the Oriente reaching extremely remote villages. The trails are not often used as small aircraft are the main means of communication with Macas, and river travel is used between the villages. I did find, however, one trail which can easily be walked in a day from Macas.

From Macas cross the Río Upano by a simple bridge to Sevilla Don Bosco, a Salesian mission. From here, head south along the road roughly following the eastern river bank. This dirt road slowly deteriorates into a wide track impassable to vehicles. You will pass cultivated areas and Indian huts and perhaps be invited to try some of their yucca chicha. This drink is made by the women masticating the yucca and then spitting the contents into a bowl of water which is left to ferment, the process started by the ptyalin in saliva. It takes some time (and a lack of imagination) to develop a taste for this sour, gruel-like drink which is served cold in large gourds. One is normally expected to drink the whole gourd in one or two large gulps.

Some four hours from Sevilla Don Bosco you come to the small Indian centre of San Luis where you can buy soft drinks if you're not up to chicha. San Luis is almost the halfway point to Sucúa but when I was there a bridge had washed out further along the trail so I returned the way I came. Either way it is a good day hike. If you do get all the way to Sucúa you could return to Macas by one of the frequent buses joining the two towns.

148

CHAPTER 8
THE WESTERN LOWLANDS

INTRODUCTION
West of the Andes and stretching to the Pacific Ocean lies some o
Ecuador's most valuable agricultural land. Although this is good fo
the Ecuadorian economy, it means also that much of the lowlan
forest has been destroyed, along with the accompanying wildlife. Th
best places to see the western forests are the slopes of the Andes
here the terrain is too rough for agriculture. Few trails have been cu
and the area is not really conducive to backpacking trips, being hot
humid, thickly covered with vegetation, and lacking the interest o
volcanoes to climb. It is, however, excellent for birdwatching.

For the naturalist, there is the interest of the prolific birdlife an
also the ecological changes as one descends from highlands to th
coast. The best centre for bird watching in the western lowlands i
Tinalandia. Lying about 800 m above sea level on the road to Sant
Domingo de los Colorados (some 15 km before the town), Tinalandi
is a beautiful guest house run by Tina and Alfredo Garzon. Th
grounds are extensive and kept in their natural state for optimum
birdwatching. There are many nature trails and over 150 species o
birds have been recorded here, including chestnut-mandibled tou
cans, pale-mandibled araçaris, and a variety of parrots, humming
birds, motmots, tanagers and other tropical species. The accommo
dation is comfortable and the food of gourmet quality, so this is no
for the budget traveller. It is also very popular with groups so yo
may have difficulty in finding a room. (There is no phone so the only
way of making a reservation is by writing. Letters addressed t
Tinalandia, Santo Domingo de los Colorados, Ecuador will reacl
there.)

A good variety of sea and shore birds is found on the coast
The southern coast has mangrove swamps but is nevertheless rathe
scrubby and dry, as is the Santa Elena peninsula west of Guayaquil
Rainfall here is comparatively low and falls mainly from January t
April. Further north there is more rainfall, more vegetation, and
longer rainy season, from January to June, and on the far norther

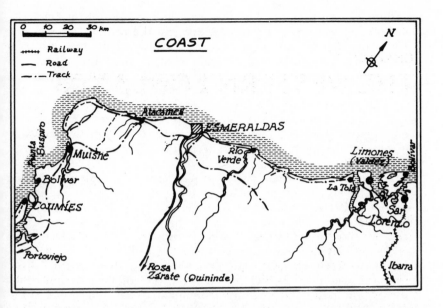

coast it sometimes rains during the 'dry' season. Good areas for bird-watching in the south are found at Jambelí, which is a low-lying island off Puerto Bolívar, near Machala, the capital of the province of El Oro. From Machala frequent buses do the short trip to Puerto Bolívar where motor boats can be hired to cruise among the swamps, estuaries, and islands of the area where you can see large flocks of pelicans and other sea birds. In the Santa Elena peninsula are found many fishing villages and tourist resorts, such as Playas and Salinas. These are often used as bases for walks along the beach although overnight backpacking trips aren't normally done.

The northern coast is perhaps richest in coastal birdlife because of the heavier rainfall and vegetation. I did a hike along part of the coast here. There are also various resort towns you can use as a base.

ANDES TO COAST BY TRAIN, CANOE, BUS, AND FOOT
The most popular route to the coast is probably by bus via Santa Domingo to either Esmeraldas or Bahía de Caráquez, but the train is much more fun and passes through remote areas unaffected by a constant stream of traffic. There are two lines; one from Quito via Riobamba to Guayaquil and a shorter one linking Ibarra with San Lorenzo on the northern coast. The 464 km Quito–Guayaquil line reaches a height of 3609 m and is a marvel of railway engineering. At one point it climbs nearly 300 m in less than 80 km and includes complex loops and switchbacks – a must for a railway enthusiast. An

excellent description of the ride is found in the *South American Handbook*. I personally prefer the 293 km Ibarra–San Lorenzo line because you detrain in a sleepy coastal port with only boat and train connections, rather than in the huge bustling port of Guayaquil.

The train is known locally as *autoferro* and is little more than a converted schoolbus mounted on a railway chassis. When I took it from Ibarra to San Lorenzo the journey, which usually takes 7 hours, lasted 12. We were stopped by two minor landslides, which, by all accounts, was par for the course. The train is accompanied throughout much of its memorable descent by the Río Mira which provides exciting whitewater views.

Once in San Lorenzo (where there are only basic hotels and restaurants) you continue down the coast by dugout canoe through Limones (officially known as Valdéz) to La Tola, some 2 hours away. This is a fascinating trip past mangrove swamps with opportunities to see pelicans galore, as well as ospreys and frigate birds. The Cayapa Indians live in the area and sometimes come into Limones, particularly at weekends. Unfortunately, they have recently been swept by an epidemic which has affected 60% of the population and leads to blindness. Attempts are being made to halt the spread of the disease, but these have not been very successful because of lack of funds, the isolation of the villages, and the lack of medical knowledge about the causes of the illness.

Occasionally boats go from San Lorenzo directly to Esmeraldas, but normally you have to catch a bus from La Tola for the 4 hour journey on to Esmeraldas. This takes you through lush coastal pastureland with good viewing of egrets, herons, and wading birds. I persuaded the driver to let me sit on the roof which made the hot trip very pleasant – but be careful of sunburn!

Once in Esmeraldas most people continue by bus to Atacames, a popular seaside resort with good beaches and many hotels. A further 30 km by rough dirt road brings you to Muisne, which is a very quiet resort with cabins on the beach and fewer tourists. Muisne is located on an island with a frequent ferry service. From Muisne you can continue south on foot along the beach to Cojimíes; this is a good coastal walk. At low tide, curious open sided buses or pickup trucks speed up and down the hard packed sand, so if you get fed up with walking you can flag one down – they pass every hour or so.

MUISNE TO COJIMÍES   From the cabins at the Muisne seafront walk south along the beach for about 5 km to the end of the island. There will be a motorized dugout canoe to ferry you across the Río Muisne for a few sucres. On the other side of the river go upstream to the tiny settlement of Las Manchas, less than a kilometre away, where there is a huddle of houses and a very small store. Walk through the village and continue along a track on the other side which leads to the coast less than a kilometre away. (If you want to avoid Las Manchas you can just follow the coast.) About 7 km of walking will bring you to the tiny coastal village of Mompiche where there is a poorly stocked store which is often closed. A headland (Punta Suspiro) blocks the beach walk, but a sandy vehicle track goes over the headland and through coastal pastureland which is absolutely teeming with birdlife. You arrive at the Portete Estuary about 4 km away where there will again be a dugout canoe waiting to ferry you across for a few sucres.

Now you have to get to the next town of Bolívar. Dugout canoes will take you there up the Portete Estuary. Or you can just cross the river and walk through a few hundred metres of streams and mangroves to the village of Portete where there is the usual ill-stocked, rarely open store. From here you can walk 6 km along the coast around Punta Bolívar and on to Bolívar. The vegetation is very thick and comes right down to the high tide mark so this section must be done at low tide.

Getting from Muisne to Bolívar involves about 22 km of walking. This can be cut down by taking a boat from Portete to Bolívar or by taking a ride on the occasional vehicles along the beach between Muisne and Portete. Carry plenty of water as the rivers aren't very clean or fresh. Sun protection is essential on the sandy, unshaded beaches. Don't forget problem areas like the backs of your legs.

Once in Bolívar you'll find several small stores where you can buy drinks. I couldn't find a hotel but you could probably persuade someone to give you a place to sleep. The best advice is to leave Muisne at dawn (which gives you a couple of cool walking hours) and arrive in Bolívar in early afternoon. It is then easy to find a boat to Cojimíes, about 8 km due south. (There are passenger boats, but don't charter a boat for yourself unless you are desperate. People will encourage you to do so but this is expensive.) This sea trip takes about 30 minutes. Cojimíes is a fishing village with one basic and unsigned hotel which you will have to ask for. There are simple restaurants and friendly people. It is off the beaten tourist track and a good place to spend the night (or two).

From Cojimíes you can continue south to San Vicente by beach bus. The open sided buses are well ventilated(!), the views are good, and the journey takes about 5 hours. This section is less suited to walking as there are much longer distances between villages and little water. San Vicente is a good beach resort, joined by ferry with Bahía de Caráquez from where you can get buses to anywhere.
(WARNING. Rain during the wet months may cause delays.)

MAPS There are two IGM maps of this area. The 1:50,000 Muisne topographical map covers from Muisne to just before Mompiche and the 1:50,000 Cojimíes planametric map shows from Mompiche to Cojimíes. To get these maps requires a special permit at the IGM.

ECUADOR FACT BOX

Size
283,520 sq km (second smallest republic in South America). 685 km from north to south.

Population
8,945,000 (1982 census).
40% Indian, 40% mestizo, 10% European, 10% others.
51% of the population live on the coastal plain, 46% in the Andean sierra and 3% in the eastern lowlands (the Oriente).
Population growth 3.3% per annum.
Population density 30 per sq km (highest in S. America).

Main Towns
Quito. The capital, in the highlands.
Population 881,000.
Guayaquil. Largest city and main port. Population 1,600,000.
Cuenca. Main town of southern highlands. Population 151,000.

History
1527 First Spanish contact; Pizarro's men land at Esmeraldas, in northern Ecuador.
1535 Incorporated into the viceroyalty of Peru; Ecuador is known as the Audiencia de Quito.
1822 Ecuador gains independence from Spain after the battle of Pichincha, May 24, under the leadership of Mariscal Sucre.
Incorporated into Gran Colombia.
1830 Becomes fully independent under first president, Juan Flores.
1981 Democratically elected President Jaime Roldós Aguilera killed in air crash. Vice President Osvaldo Hurtado Larrea assumes power.
1984 Democratic elections.

Weather
Quito rainy season: September–May; average annual rainfall 1270 mm. Mean temperature 13°C; average high temperature 22°C, average low temperature 7°C. Guayaquil rainy season: December–May. Average high temperature 32°C, average low temperature 20°C.

Holidays

Jan 1	New Year's Day	Aug 10	Quito Independence Day
Moveable	Epiphany		
Moveable	Carnival (Monday & Tuesday before Lent)	Oct 9	Guayaquil Independence Day
Moveable	Holy Thursday, Good Friday, Holy Saturday, Easter Sunday	Oct 12	Columbus Day
		Nov 1	All Saints Day
		Nov 2	All Souls Day
May 1	Labour Day	Nov 3	Cuenca Independence Day
May 24	Battle of Pichincha	Dec 6	Foundation of Quito
July 24	Bolívar's Birthday		

APPENDIX A – ELEVATIONS

The height of a mountain is a constant source of interest to laymen and climbers alike. Upon returning from a climb, one is often asked "How high is it?" before being questioned about the difficulty, duration, or equipment needed for the ascent. In lesser known areas, the question "How high is it?" is not easily answered. Maps are often sketchy or inaccurate, and different sources come up with various possible heights for the same mountain. Perhaps one of these is correct, perhaps none.

For the sake of consistency, I have used what appears to be the most accurate source for the elevations in this book. These are from the 1979 Instituto Geográfico Militar (IGM) 1:500,000 map of Ecuador. Many other sources are available, and even different maps from the Institute have a variety of elevations. The following table lists various given elevations of Ecuador's major peaks.

SOURCES
1. Instituto Geográfico Militar 1:500,000 map, 1979.
2. IGM 1:1,000,000 map, 1981.
3. IGM 1:50,000 series maps, various years.
4. *Montaña* magazine; Colegio San Gabriel, Quito. No. 11, June 1975.
5. *The Fool's Climbing Guide To Ecuador and Peru* by Michael Koerner, 1976.
6. *El Volcanismo en El Ecuador* by Minard L. Hall, 1977.

	1	2	3	4	5	6	7
Chimborazo	6310	6310	6310	6310	6310	6267	6270
Cotopaxi*	5897	5897	5880+	6005	5897	5897	5896
Cayambe	5790	5790	—	5840	5790	5790	5796
Antisana*	5704	5705	5753	5750	5704	5705	5704
El Altar*	5319	5319	—	5404	5404	5319	5270
Iliniza Sur	5263	5263	5248	5305	5305	5266	5304
Sangay*	5230	5230	—	5323	5230	5230	5230
Iliniza Norte	—	—	5126	5116	5116	—	—
Carihuairazo	5020	5020	—	5106	5116	4990	—
Tungurahua*	5016	5016	—	5087	5016	5016	5033
Cotacachi	4939	4937	—	4966	4939	4939	4940
Sincholagua	4893	4899	4893	4988	4893	4898	—
Quilindaña	4878	4878	4760+	4919	4878	4898	—
Guagua Pichincha*	4874	4794	4784	4850	4839	4794	4794
Corazón	4788	4788	4788	4810	4788	4786	—
Chiles	4768	4764	4768	4720	4712	4720	—
Rumiñahui	4712	4712	4712	4757	4712	4722	—
Rucu Pichincha	—	—	4680+	4787	4787	4698	—
Sara Urco	4676	4676	—	4725	4710	—	—
Imbabura	4609	—	4560	4630	4630	4630	—
Hermoso	4571	4571	—	—	4571	—	—
Puntas	4452	4452	—	—	—	4452	—
Atacazo	4410	4457	4463	4470	4457	4457	—
Pasochoa	4200	4200	4199	4220	4255	4199	—
Sumaco*	3900	3900	—	3828	3828	3828	—
Reventador*	3485	3485	—	3485	3485	3485	3485

All heights are in metres.
* signifies active or potentially active volcanoes.
Elevations used in this book are shown in heavy type.

APPENDIX B — SPANISH VOCABULARY

With the exception of a few small, remote, lowland Indian groups everyone speaks Spanish in Ecuador, including the Andean Indians, although for them it is a second language after Quechua. Other European languages are rarely understood except in the major tourist agencies and first class hotels. Therefore it is essential that you learn some basic Spanish; take heart, it is an easy language to learn.

Quechua, though widely spoken in the highlands, is a difficult language to learn and dialects tend to vary greatly from area to area. So unless you are an avid linguist you're better off learning some Spanish.

The following list of words and phrases will get you started:

USEFUL PHRASES

Where are you going?	*A donde va?*
Where are you coming from?	*De donde viene?*
I'm passing through	*Estoy paseando.*
Can I camp?	*Puedo acampar?*
Where is the trail to ...?	*Donde está el camino por ....?*
How are you?	*Como está?*

GENERAL VOCABULARY

Bad.	*Malo*	No	*No*
Baggage	*Equipaje*	Pickup truck	*Camioneta*
Bath	*Baño*	Please	*Por favor*
Bus.	*Bus, colectivo*	Road.	*Carretera*
Good	*Bueno*	Room (in hotel)	*Habitación*
Good morning/day	*Buenos días*	Thank-you	*Gracias*
Good afternoon	*Buenas tardes*	Train.	*Ferrocarril, tren*
Good evening/night	*Buenas noches*	Yes.	*Sí*
Goodbye	*Adios*		

CLIMBERS AND HIKERS VOCABULARY

Above	*Arriba*	Landslide	*Derrumbe*
Altitude	*Altura*	Left	*Izquierda*
Aqueduct	*Acequia*	Meadow	*Pampa*
Ascent	*Subida*	Moraine	*Morena*
Backpack	*Mochila*	Mountain (with-	*Cerro*
Below	*Abajo*	out snow)	
Bivouac	*Vivac*	Mountain (snow	*Nevado*
Boots (climbing)	*Botas (de andinismo)*	peak)	
Bridge	*Puente*	Mountaineer	*Andinista*
Camp	*Campamento*	Mule	*Mula*
Carabiners	*Mosquetones*	Muleteer	*Arriero*
Climb (down)	*Bajar*	Needle	*Aguja*
Climb (up)	*Escalar, Ascender*	North	*Norte*
Close (to)	*Cerca*	Pass	*Paso, Abra, Porta-*
Cold	*Frio*		*chuelo, Punta*
Crampons	*Grampones*	Peak	*Pico*
Crevasse	*Grieta*	Plain (plateau)	*Pampa*
(to) Cross	*Cruzar, Atravesar*	Point (minor	*Punta*
Distant	*Lejos*	peak)	
East	*Este*	Rain	*Lluvia*
Face	*Cara*	Ravine	*Quebrada*
Fixed rope	*Cuerda fija*	Right	*Derecha*
Fog	*Niebla*	River	*Río*
Forest	*Bosque*	Rock	*Roca*
Freeze	*Congelar*	Rope	*Cuerda, Soga*
Glacier	*Glaciar*	Route	*Ruta*
Hail	*Granizo*	Snow	*Nieve*
Hammer	*Martillo*	South	*Sur*
Highlands	*Sierra*	Straight ahead	*Derecho, Recto*
Hill	*Loma*	Summit	*Cima, Cumbre*
House	*Casa*	Swamp	*Pantano*
Hut (climbers')	*Refugio*	Tent	*Carpa*
Ice	*Hielo*	Trail	*Sendero*
Ice Axe	*Piolet*	Valley	*Valle*
Ice Screw	*Tornillo*	Village	*Pueblo*
Lake	*Lago, Laguna*	Waterfall	*Cascada*
		West	*Oeste*

APPENDIX C – MEASUREMENTS AND CONVERSIONS

Latin America uses metric measurements and so have I throughout this book
These conversion formulae and tables should help you.

Many people will want to convert metres to the more familiar feet. If you
remember that 3 metres is 0.84 feet, or just under 10 feet, you can do an app
roximate conversion quickly: to convert heights shown in metres to feet, divide
by 3 and add a zero, e.g. 6,000 m = 20,000 feet.

The error is only 1.5%.

CONVERSION FORMULAE

To convert	Multiply by
Inches to centimetres	2.540
Centimetres to inches	0.3937
Feet to Metres	0.3048
Metres to feet	3.281
Yards to metres	0.9144
Metres to yards	1.094
Miles to kilometres	1.609
Kilometres to miles	0.6214
Acres to hectares	0.4047
Hectares to acres	2.471
Imperial gallons to litres	4.546
Litres to imperial gallons	0.22
US gallons to litres	3.785
Litres to U.S. gallons	0.264
Ounces to grams	28.35
Grams to ounces	0.03527
Pounds to grams	453.6
Grams to pounds	0.002205
Pounds to kilograms	0.4536
Kilograms to pounds	2.205
British tons to kilograms	1016.00
Kilograms to British tons	0.0009842
U.S. tons to kilograms	907.00
Kilograms to U.S. tons	0.000907

TEMPERATURE CONVERSION TABLE

The bold figures in the central columns can be read as either centigrade or fahrenheit.

Centigrade		Fahrenheit
−18	0	32
−15	5	41
−12	10	50
− 9	15	59
− 7	20	68
− 4	25	77
− 1	30	86
2	35	95
4	40	104
7	45	113
10	50	122
13	55	131
16	60	140
18	65	149
21	70	158
24	75	167
27	80	176
32	90	194
38	100	212
40	104	

(5 imperial gallons are equal to 6 U.S. gallons.
A British ton is 2,240 lbs. A U.S. ton is 2,000 lbs.)

BIBLIOGRAPHY

This lists all the books I referred to in preparing this guide and a few more besides. I have tried to give as much variety as possible. Many more books are available if you wish to delve more deeply.

GENERAL SOUTH AMERICAN GUIDE BOOKS

The South American Handbook edited by John Brooks. Trade and Travel Publications Ltd, Bath, England. Updated annually, this 1,400 page book is the best overall guide to Latin America. Expensive, but worth every penny to anyone planning on spending a long time in Latin America.

South America on a Shoestring by Geoff Crowther. Lonely Planet Publications, Australia. 2nd edition, May 1983. A good general guide for the budget traveller, with many city maps.

A Traveler's Guide to El Dorado and the Inca Empire: Colombia, Ecuador, Peru, Bolivia by Lynn Meisch. Penguin Books, 1977 (new edition due 1984). Particularly recommended for its detailed information on Andean Indians, their culture, traditions, clothing, markets, fiestas, handicrafts, etc., as well as useful general travel information.

"Mainstream" guides by Frommer, Waldo, Birnbaum and Fodor, the $15 or $20 a day books etc., are all right as basic guides to the continent.

GUIDEBOOKS FOR THE OUTDOORS

Backpacking in Venezuela, Colombia and Ecuador by Hilary and George Bradt. Bradt Enterprises, 1979. A backpacking guide with a more personal approach. Includes some Ecuadorian hikes not covered here and several excellent hikes in Venezuela and Colombia.

The Fool's Climbing Guide to Ecuador by Michael Koerner. Buzzard Mountaineering, U.S.A., 1976. The first English language guide to Ecuador's mountains. Not particularly detailed but its humorous descriptions make it worthwhile reading.

A Climbers and Hikers Guide to the World's Mountains by Michael R. Kelsey, 1982. Includes about 20 pages of maps and information on Ecuador and over 600 pages on the rest of the world. For the globetrotting mountaineer, this is the book.

South America: River Trips, Volume I, edited by George Bradt, 1981 and *Volume II* by Tanis and Martin Jordan, 1982. Bradt Enterprises. Volume I includes information on some Ecuadorian rivers and Volume II has an incredible wealth of background on South American river travel.

Guia Para Excursiones en Automovil a Traves del Ecuador by Arthur Weilbauer. Quito, 1979. Available in Spanish, German and English, but only the Spanish version includes a map. (This makes the English edition a bit incomprehensible, e.g. what are "Side trips from Route K"?) If you have a car, get both Spanish and English translations and you'll have an invaluable guide to all the major and most minor roads in Ecuador.

GENERAL MOUNTAINEERING AND EXPLORATION

Travels Amongst the Great Andes of the Equator by Edward Whymper, 1891; reprinted by Charles Knight in 1972, but now out of print. Worth getting hold of – this book describes the 1880 expedition which first climbed Ecuador's highest peak, and made seven other first ascents.

Personal Narrative of the Travels to the Equinoctial Regions of the New Continent by Alexander von Humboldt and Aime Bongland. Various editions. Again, difficult to find, but fascinating reading for anyone interested in the historical aspects of Latin American exploration.

Sangay Survived by Richard Snailham. Hutchinson, 1978 (now out of print). The story of a six man British scientific expedition to the volcano which ended disastrously when an eruption killed or injured most of the members.

The Next Horizon by Chris Bonington. Victor Gollancz Ltd., 1973. This autobiographical book by one of Britain's leading climbers includes two chapters on climbing Sangay.

NATURAL HISTORY AND VOLCANOLOGY

Fauna del Ecuador by Erwin Patzelt, Quito 1978. In Spanish, now out of print. A small but comprehensive book, particularly useful on mammals, though sketchy on birds and other animals.

The Andes by Tony Morrison. Time-Life Books, 1975. A beautiful book covering the whole Andean chain; Ecuador's mountains are not forgotten with superb photographs of Cotopaxi and Sangay.

Land Above the Clouds by Tony Morrison. Deutsch, 1974. This book also deals with the whole Andean chain with an emphasis on its wildlife. Recommended.

The Flight of the Condor by Michael Andrews. Collins, 1982. Subtitled *A Wildlife Exploration of the Andes* this well-illustrated book contains an excellent chapter on Ecuador.

Ecuador: Snow Peaks and Jungles by Arthur Eichler, English translation, Cromwell, N.Y., 1955. Also bilingual edition by Eichler, Quito 1970.

Although some of the information is rather inaccurate, the excellent photographs make this a book well worth looking at.

Ecuador – In the Shadow of the Volcanoes, Ediciones Libri Mundi, 1981. Available in English, Spanish, German and French. A "coffee-table" book, with many superb photos.

El Volcanismo en El Ecuador by Minard L. Hall. I.P.G.H., Quito, 1977. In Spanish, mainly of interest to the volcanologist – the best work on the subject.

ORNITHOLOGY *(My thanks to Paul Greenfield, bird illustrator and expert on Ecuadorian species, for help in preparing this exhaustive list.)*

A Guide to the Birds of Ecuador by R. Ridgely and P. Greenfield. Princeton University Press. Expected c. 1988. One of a series, this definitive book will illustrate and describe every Ecuadorian species, including those on the Galapagos. Other books in this series are:

A Guide to the Birds of Panama by R. Ridgely. Princeton University Press, 1976. An excellent book, of use in the coastal regions of Ecuador.

A Guide to the Birds of Venezuela by R.M. de Schauensee, W.H. Phelps Jr., and G. Tudor. Princeton University Press, 1978. Particularly useful for the Oriente, but has some inaccuracies.

A Guide to the Birds of Colombia by Brown and Hilty. Princeton University Press, expected 1984/85. This book will probably cover about 80% of Ecuadorian species.

The Birds of Ecuador and the Galapagos Archipelago by Thomas Y Butler. Ramphastos Agen POB 1091, Portsmouth, N.H. 03801, U.S.A., 1979. Basically a check list with useful tables showing the zones in which each species is found.

A Guide to the Birds of South America by R.M. de Schauensee. Livingstone Pub. Co., Wynnewood, P.A. The only book to cover all of the nearly 3,000 birds of the continent, hence necessarily brief in its descriptions.

South American Land Birds – A Photographic Aid to Identification by John S. Dunning, Harrowood Books, Newtown Square, P.A., 1982. A new book which describes over 80% of the South American species. 1,112 are illustrated. Again, necessarily brief descriptions and does not cover sea, shore and lake birds.

MISCELLANEOUS

Ingapirca edited by Jorge Aravena. Editora Andina, Quito, 1982. A small, Spanish language guide to the ruins, with photographs, poems, and a short playing record.

El Clima y Sus Caracteristicas en El Ecuador by Carlos Blandin Landivar. I.P.G.H., Quito, 1976. A Spanish language book on the meteorology of Ecuador.

Ecuador – A Travel Journal by Henri Michaux, Peter Owen, 1970 (out of print). A book of poetry and prose describing the 1928 visit to Ecuador by a Belgian mystic, poet, and writer.

The Lost World of the Aucas by K.D. Gertelmann. Quito, 1977. A multi-lingual book with many colour photographs describing one of the least known and least accessible Indian tribes of Ecuador.

Humboldt and the Cosmos by Douglas Botting. Sphere Books, London. A biographical account of one of the best known early explorers of Ecuador and South America.

Medicine for Mountaineering by James A. Wilkerson, M.D. The Mountaineers, Seattle, 1975. A standard reference.

Mountaineering Medicine – A Wilderness Medical Guide by Fred T. Darvill, M.D. Skagit Mountain Rescue, POB 2, Mt. Vernon, WA 98273, U.S.A. A small booklet useful for carrying on hiking and climbing trips.

The Conquest of the Incas by John Hemming. Macmillan 1970. Penguin 1983. A thorough and exceptional work on the subject.

PERIODICALS

Montaña The magazine of the San Gabriel Climbing Club, Quito. The oldest established mountaineering magazine in Ecuador, appearing at irregular intervals (No. 11, January 1975, No. 12, January 1980, No. 13, July 1981, No. 14, April 1983). In Spanish with some English mountain descriptions.

Campo Abierto Quito, Ecuador. A small mountaineering magazine begun in 1982; latest edition No. 5, March 1983. Spanish language.

INDEX

ABOUT THE AUTHOR

Rob Rachowiecki has been exploring wilderness areas in various parts of the world since the age of sixteen. He has travelled overland from Alaska to Tierra del Fuego and now works as an adventure travel guide in South America. This is his second book.

1987 ADDENDA

My thanks to readers and climbing friends (Alan Miller, Tom Hunt, Sarah Lockland, Geof Bartram, Martin Slater, M.Whittam, and Tim Boyer) who have written to tell me of changes in Ecuador and pointing out errors. I hope you will continue to send in updates. Even though a new edition may not be due for a while, the latest changes are always available (for a small charge) in the form of a computer printout from the publisher, so anyone about to do a serious expedition to Ecuador would do well to write (enclosing a s.a.e) for the latest climbing and hiking news.

Rob Rachowiecki

☆   ☆   ☆

	HISTORY
Page 18	Sorry, a mix-up of nationalities here. Joseph Bergé was French (now dead) and James Desrossiers is American.

	GETTING THERE
Page 19	The airport departure tax is now $5.

	MONEY MATTERS
Page 24	In 1987 there were about 150 sucres to the US dollar.

	TRANSPORT
Page 35	In 1987, trains between Guayaquil and Riobamba were not running due to 80km of railway being washed away in the 1983 *El Niño.*.

	SECURITY
Page 36	Some climber friends recently had everything but their tent stolen from the Italian base camp on El Altar whilst they were scouting Obispo. So always leave someone to guard the camp. If your entire group wants to climb, I suggest you hire a local *arriero* or muleman to look after your gear.

RENTING EQUIPMENT

Page 38
M.Whittam, from the Bahamas, writes 'Yanasacha, the climbing shop, is closed. Almacen Cotopaxi did not prove useful. They refused to sell us one of the two ropes they had in the shop, and we ended up buying a rope from a group of Colombian climbers at the Gran Casino. So I would advise anyone to take a rope with them.'

PICHINCHAS

Page 63
In 1983 a hut was built on Guagua Pichincha by the Ministry of Civil Defence. It is above the village of Lloa on the south side about half an hour below the summit and crater. Although the hut is mainly used by scientists, the caretaker will normally allow small groups of climbers to stay the night.

RUCU PICHINCHA

Page 66
A new owner of the *hacienda* half way up the hill closed the access road to private vehicles recently. Sometimes the road is open, but you can't rely on it. By law, it must be open to walkers.

If you don't want to follow those white arrows painted on rocks, the summit via the easier sandy slopes takes about 1½ hours to reach from the trail junction. The rock route is more direct although perhaps a little hair-raising for beginners. The rock is solid because this is a popular route and gets many day ascents from Quito, so all the loose rock gets tossed off. The first few metres onto the rocky ridge are the most difficult. Once you're on the ridge you'll find that the rock has been worn a lighter colour along the main ascent route. Almost an hour into the climb there's a narrow section which you have to climb down to. It's only a metre wide and rather exposed so beginners may want a short rope here, though experienced climbers won't have any difficulty. From here it's about 20 minutes to the top. There is some more rock climbing to be had on Rucu's summit pyramid if you are so inclined — experienced rock climbers will find their own route.

TRANSPORT TO GUAGUA

Page 67
An ordinary pick-up truck can sometimes be hired in Lloa which can get you within 3 hours walk of the scientists' hut. If you bring a four wheel drive vehicle from Quito you can get within about 200m of the hut. In a vehicle (or on foot) follow the road past the church, past a sign for Granja Ovina, past a right hand fork until you reach a Y junction about 4km from Lloa. Here you take the right fork. About 4km further up, a flat area is used for parking. From here continue on a rough track (on foot or with four wheel drive vehicles only) heading more or less

north to the hut and the summit. There are no technical problems and the round trip could be done (on foot) in a long day from Lloa.

From the scientists' hut you could return to Quito via Rucu Pichincha in one long day. It's a beautiful hike because the west side of Rucu has a large variety of flowering plants. From the hut traverse north then east. Follow the ridge past Padre Encantado and then climb up a basin that looks steep and long with a lot of loose rock. It's much easier than it looks and takes about half an hour to climb. Rucu is just beyond. If you look carefully you'll be able to follow a faint path for most of the way.

ILINIZA SUR

The normal route is via the left (east) side of the north face. From the Nuevos Horizontes hut (reported by M.Whittam to be in a bad state, with the door not closing, dirty, and the surrounding area and water supply full of garbage) head a few hundred metres west into the saddle between the north and south mountains. Look for two large rock outcrops and find a snow ramp which begins below and to the left of them. Climb this snow ramp, angling right and then follow the east ridge to the summit, traversing below the rocky outcrop known as *el hongo* (the mushroom). The descent is via the same route. Usually some crevasses have to be negotiated (often you can climb round them). In good conditions the round trip can be done in 5 to 6 hours but a full day is not uncommon. Therefore you should plan a pre-dawn departure to minimise rockfall and avalanche danger caused by the melting of the snow in the midday sun. The 40 degree descent can be hazardous in soft snow for inexperienced climbers because it tends to ball up underneath your crampons.

A more difficult route still was done by Marco Cruz and Joseph Bergé in October 1973 and goes up the south ridge. A bivouac and highly technical ice climbing were required. The route was repeated by Martin Slater, Travis White and Peter Hall in March 1974 and again by George Gibson and Allan Miller in June 1977.

Tom Hunt reports a new route on the southwest face climbed by himself, and Jorge and Delia Montpoli in September 1982. This route is approached from the 3600 m Loma de Huinza pass on the Sigchos road, south of the mountain. Head for the base of the westernmost glacier located just north of the prominent, crumbling rock towers that divide the south and west sides of the mountain (8 hours). Camp here. Climb the left side of the heavily crevassed glacier to a 40 degree snow ramp which bears further left and above the first rock walls. Ascend a steep couloir to the right (75 degrees, 50 m) and at the top angle right along a a mild ridge to a 5 m ice wall. Ascend the final 100m to the summit via the southwest knife ridge. Total climbing time from camp was 5 hours for 900m of ascent.

CHIMBORAZO

Page 80

Unless there has been snow recently, the rock band can be difficult. Several snow/ice gullies offer access through the rock band but without recent snow you can expect thin, hard, steep ice in the gullies. One of the central gullies is the easiest; the angle is about fifty degrees and so front pointing will be needed. If these gullies prove too difficult, you can head to the right and around the corner and try ascending a short steep gully of loose rock. Above the rock band is a fairly steep snow-field which is best climbed by zigzagging. Towards the top of this snow-field there is another large rock band to your right, but the route traverses under seracs to the left hand horizon. The top of the snowfield and the traverse are usually marked with flags and footprints. There is considerable objective danger from ice fall from the seracs above the traverse. The traverse has the added danger of slab avalanches, particularly after new snowfall and high winds. You are therefore advised to cross this area as quickly as possible and use caution.

M.Whittam writes 'The new Whymper Route on Chimborazo now has Refugios (both with guardians). The new lower one is very luxurious, as mountain huts go, and beer, cigarettes, sweets and soft drinks can be bought there and a jeep or pick-up truck can get there very easily, leaving only a 20 minute walk to the Whymper hut.

'When we climbed Chimborazo, we followed the wands which did not traverse left under the seracs, but went straight up — it became very steep (70 degrees) with poor ice under 6 inches of snow — not for beginners.'

CAYAMBE

Page 90

Do not attempt to climb or descend the snowfield beneath the summit unless it is still early enough in the day for the snow to be frozen. You should be below it by about 11am at the latest on your descent which means a midnight wake up is not unreasonable.

COTOPAXI

Page 104

From Plaza Chile the trip into Cotopaxi will cost around US $20 (bargaining expected) but make sure you specify that you want to get to the parking lot under the *refugio* because many drivers won't or can't go that far. One driver who does the trip is named Manuel Rodriguez.

Recently it has been easier to avoid the triangular scree slope above the hut, and instead to head up to the right from the hut, traversing around the mountain and either climbing up the first glacier you reach or crossing it and continuing to the second, larger glacier and climbing it. Whichever way you go, you'll be passing the big black rock outcrop known as Yanasacha well to the right and then coming back to the left to reach the summit crater. The last 200 m or so are quite steep. However, much the route changes, you'll find a fairly well defined trail consisting of cairns, marker wands, and footprints left by the many groups which climb this mountain. Ascents are made almost every weekend and frequently mid-week also.

TUNGURAHUA

Page 115

As of 1986 there is a hut being built just above Pondoa where there are plans to collect a park fee. The new road now reaches this point and there is a truck service run by Sr. Vicente Sanchez M. who can be contacted through Pension Patty. He charges about a dollar per person and can arrange mules to meet you at the trailhead for about US $4 per mule. He doesn't run this service on Sundays and Mondays. He is also available for other transport such as to El Altar — about US $60 round trip for a truck full of people. You should be aware of the fact that the hut can be overcrowded at weekends and holidays — in excess of 50 people have been reported. You may want to bring a tent at these times.

Vicente Sanchez has a truck which gets into El Altar from Baños.

OBISPO

Page 119

The rock wall below the summit has been graded about 5.5 on the Yosemite Decimal System or Grade IV UIAA. The climb involves forty degree snow, when there is snow. In the mid 1980s much of the snow has melted and the climbing is hard rock. To avoid the first gully, one can climb to the upper glacier on the ridge to the right. After crossing the lower glacier, go under the ridge and then up and around on the western side. Go up a snow gully and get on the ridge, staying just below the ridge crest on the snow ledges until you reach the upper glacier, then continue with the Italian Route. This is known as the Japanese Route (I have also seen it called the Calvary Ridge Route) and is used as the standard descent route. Rappels are sometimes used (Page 120) for the descent. Further around the corner from the Japanese Route is the more difficult Superior Glacier Route. Looking up, you'll see a steep snow slope, with an ice cliff with long icicles on the left and crevasses to the right. The climb begins with three or four pitches of forty degree climbing but it finishes nearly vertical, topping out onto the upper, or superior, glacier.

REVENTADOR

Page 141   There are some local guides available and it is suggested you hire someone. This is because the dense vegetation makes the trail very difficult to follow if nobody has been in for a couple of months and it's easy to get lost in an impenetrable tangle of brush. There is little water. The most experienced guide is Guillermo Vasquez who was involved in chopping the original trail and who knows the area well. He lives by the school in the Pampas area some 2 or 3 kms before you get to Rio Reventador from Quito. Jorge and Segundo are less experienced. The most difficult part of trail finding is the first hour or two. Local woodcutters keep cutting new trails which makes things confusing. Once you're past the logging area it's a little easier to follow the trail.

BIBLIOGRAPHY

Page 158   *A Guide to the Birds of Colombia* was published in 1986 and is excellent (though expensive).

ESPAÑOL EN ECUADOR

* Bet you can't find a more efficient and inexpensive way to learn Spanish!

* Specially designed programs for foreign students

* 7 hours daily of individual instruction (one-to-one with teacher). Monday through Friday

* Essentially practical courses, based on vocabulary, grammar and conversation, at all levels

* The system is self-paced and you can start at any time

* You live at the home of an Ecuadorian family where you get 3 meals, have your own bedroom and laundry service

For Further information write to:

Academia de Español Quito

Marchena Nº. 130 y 10 de Agosto — Casilla 39-C
QUITO — ECUADOR

THE TOP TEN

Peaks over 5000 metres in Ecuador

CHIMBORAZO	6310 metres	(20703 feet)
COTOPAXI	5897 metres	(19348 feet)
CAYAMBE	5790 metres	(18997 feet)
ANTISANA	5704 metres	(18715 feet)
EL ALTAR	5319 metres	(17452 feet)
ILINIZA S.	5263 metres	(17268 feet)
SANGAY	5230 metres	(17160 feet)
ILINIZA N.	5126 metres	(16818 feet)
CARIHUAIRAZO	5020 metres	(16471 feet)
TUNGURAHUA	5016 metres	(16457 feet)

OTHER BOOKS ON SOUTH AMERICA FROM BRADT PUBLICATIONS

Backpacking in Mexico and Central America by Hilary Bradt and Rob Rachowiecki.
The second edition the first book to cover the countryside of Central America in detail, with a particular emphasis on Costa Rica and its excellent national parks. Also information on climbing Mexico's volcanoes.

Backpacking in Venezuela, Colombia and Ecuador by George and Hilary Bradt.
Eleven treks in the northern Andes show you the national parks, take you into cloud forest and up to the snowline. Includes Colombia's Sierra Nevada de Santa Marta and Cocuy, Venezuela's Sierra Nevada de Mérida, and many other outstanding hikes.

Backpacking and Trekking in Peru & Bolivia
by Hilary Bradt
The 4ᵗʰ edition of our most popular book, greatly expanded to cover all the best hiking areas in these countries: the Cordilleras Blanca, Vilcanota, Vilcabamba, and Real, including the famous Inca Trail to Machu Picchu.
Maps, line drawings & photos.

Backpacking in Chile and Argentina by Hilary Bradt and John Pilkington.
The Lake Districts, Patagonia and Tierra del Fuego are some of the areas covered. Includes a pre-war guide to the Falkland Islands.

South America: River Trips by George Bradt.
A guide to river travel by cargo boat, rubber raft or canoe, with descriptions of eleven rivers including the Amazon.

Up the Creek by John Harrison.
An exciting account of a canoe trip up one of Brazil's least explored rivers — the Jari.

This is just a selection of the books and maps for adventurous travellers that we stock. Send for our latest catalogue.

Bradt Publications, 41 Nortoft Rd, Chalfont St Peter, Bucks SL9 0LA, England

Some of the above books are available from Hunter Publishing, USA.

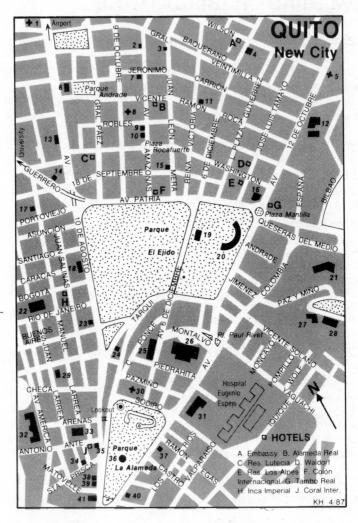

KEY FOR QUITO MAP (NEW CITY)

1. Iglesia Sta. Clara de San Millán
2. Turismundial
3. Libri Mundi
4. Ministry of Public Works
5. Iglesia El Girón
6. Ministry of External Relations
7. Bank of London & South America
8. Iglesia Santa Teresa
9. Casa de cambio 'Rodrigo Paz'
10. Ecuadorian Tours (Amex)
11. DITURIS (Tourist Office)
12. Universidad Católica (museums)
13. Ministry of Finance
14. Expresso Turismo (bus)
15. Casa de cambio 'Unicambios'
16. United States Embassy
17. Flota Imbabura (bus)
18. Immigration; Dept. of Social Security
19. Cultural Library
20. Casa de la Cultura
21. Nuevo Hospital Militar
22. Colegio Militar
23. Banco Holandés Unido
24. Alitalia
25. Palacio de Justicia
26. Palacio Legislativo
27. Instituto Panamericano de Geografía y Historia
28. Instituto Geográfico Militar (IGM)
29. Ministry of Public Health
30. Iglesia El Belén
31. Maternity Hospital
32. Colegio Mejía (museum)
33. Consejo Provincial de Pichincha
34. Banco Internacional
35. First National City Bank
36. Astronomical Observatory
37. Ciné Capitol
38. TAME
39. Banco de los Andes
40. SAETA and Red Cross
41. Banco Central (museums)

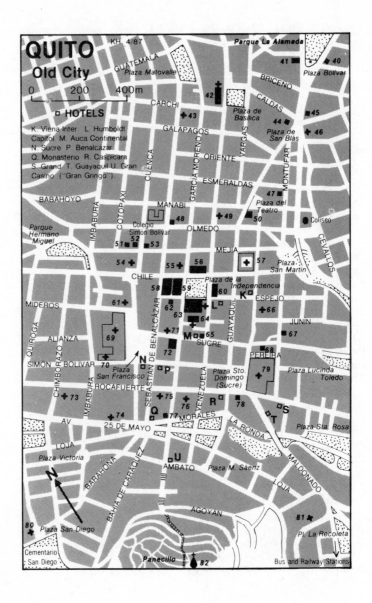

QUITO
Old City

KH 4/87

0   200   400m

□ HOTELS

K. Viena Inter. L. Humboldt
Capitol M. Auca Continental
N. Sucre P. Benalcázar
Q. Monasterio R. Caspicara
S. Grand T. Guayaquil U. Gran
Casino ("Gran Gringo")

GUATEMALA
Plaza Matovalle
CARCHI
GALAPAGOS
ORIENTE
ESMERALDAS
CUENCA
MANABI
Colegio
Simón Bolívar
OLMEDO
CHILE
MEJIA
BABAHOYO
IMBABURA
COTOPAXI
GARCIA MORENO
VARGAS
Parque
Hermano
Miguel
MIDEROS
QUIROGA
ALIANZA
SIMON BOLIVAR
CHIMBORAZO
IMBABURA
ROCAFUERTE
AV
25 DE MAYO
LOJA
Plaza Victoria
BARAHONA
BAHIA DE CARAQUEZ
AMBATO
AGOYAN
Plaza San Diego
Cementario
San Diego
Panecillo

Parque La Alameda
Plaza Bolívar
BRICENO
CALDAS
Plaza de
Basílica
Plaza de
San Blas
MONTUFAR
CEVALLOS
Plaza del
Teatro
Coliseo
Plaza
San Martín
Plaza de la
Independencia
ESPEJO
JUNIN
GUAYAQUIL
SUCRE
PEREIRA
Plaza Lucinda
Toledo
Plaza Sto.
Domingo
(Sucre)
VENEZUELA
LA RONDA
Plaza Sta. Rosa
MORALES
MALDONADO
Plaza M. Sáenz
LOJA
Pl. La Recoleta
Bus and Railway Stations

SEBASTIAN DE BENALCÁZAR
Plaza
San Francisco

N

KEY FOR QUITO MAP (OLD CITY)

42. The Basilica
43. Iglesia San Juan
44. Ciné Alhambra
45. Ministry of Agriculture
46. Iglesia de San Blás
47. Ciné Central
48. Instituto Ecuatoriano de Cultura Hispánica
49. Iglesia de Carmen Bajo
50. Teatro Sucre
51. Academy of History
52. Museum of Colonial Art
53. National Art Museum
54. Basilica de La Merced
55. Iglesia de la Concepción
56. Archbishop's Palace
57. Iglesia de San Agustín (and museum)
58. General Post Office
59. Government Palace
60. Municipal Palace (inc. Tourist Office)
61. Templo Evangélico
62. Municipal Museum of Art and History
63. Cathedral
64. El Sagrario chapel
65. Casa de Sucre (museum)
66. Iglesia de Santa Catalina
67. Ciné Rumiñahui
68. Flota Imbabura (bus)
69. San Francisco: Church, monastery and museum
70. Catuña chapel
71. Iglesia de la Compañia
72. National Library
73. Iglesia San Roque
74. El Robo chapel
75. Convent of Carmen Alto
76. Hospital Chapel of San Juan de Dios
77. Transportes Esmeraldas (bus)
78. Ministry of Public Education
79. Iglesia de Santo Domingo (museum)
80. Iglesia San Diego (Convent and museum)
81. Iglesia San Sebastián
82. Panecillo lookout and restaurant

NOTES

NOTES

NOTES

ECUADOR

0   50   100
km

Tumaco

C. Manglares
B. de Ancón
de Sardinas
San Lorenzo
Limones

Barbacoas
La Unión

COLOMBIA

San Agustín
Pitalito
El Doncello
Pto. Rico
Florencia
La Montañita
Belén

Junín
Vol. de Galeras
Tuquerres
Ibiales
Pasto
Mocoa
Valparaiso

Esmeraldas
Pta. Galera Súa
Atacames
Ríoverde
La Tola
Selva Alegre
Lita

Nev. de Cumbal
Vol. Chiles
Tulcán
San Gabriel
Orito
Pto. Asís
Pto. Limón
Caquetá
Tres Esquinas

Ens. de Mompiche
Muisne

El Angel

San Miguel
Sta. Cecilia
Lago Agrio
Putumayo
Pto. Ospina
Pto. Leguízamo
Güeppi

Cojimíes
Pedernales

Rosa Zárate
Co. Cotacachi
Ibarra
Otavalo
Cayambe
Putumayo
Shushufindi

0°
Equator
Jama

Rucu Pichincha
Vol. Cayambe
Vol. Reventador
Aguarico
Coca
Sacha
Limoncocha
Panacocha

Bahía de
Caráquez
B. Manta
Manta
Montecristi
Portoviejo
Sta. Ana

Sto. Domingo
de los Colorados
Machachi
Co. Iliniza
Vol. Antisano
Baeza
Vol. Sumaco
Loreto
Tiputini
Tiputini

Chone
Junín
Calceta
Balzar

Saquisilí
Velasco Ibarra
Quevedo
Vol. Cotopaxi
Latacunga
Archidona
Tena
Pto. Misahualli
Pto. Napo
Nuevo Rocafuerte
Pantoja
Napo

Jipijapa
Pto. López
Manglaralto
Babahoyo
Daule
Vindes

Ambato
Vol. Chimborazo
Vol. Tungurahua
Baños
Puyo
Shell-Mera
Guaranda
Cañelos
Arajuno
Sandóval
Curaray
Arica

Sta
Elena
Salinas
Ancón
Guayaquil
Durán
Milagro
Bucay
Calabamba
Guamote
Riobamba
Chiguaza
Vol. Sangay
Conanaco

Playas
Posorja
I. de Puná
Balao
Naranjal
Puná
Alausí
Zuñac
Sibambe
Ingapirca
Macuma
Chichirota
Marsella
Corrientes
Río Tigre
Tigre

Golfo de
Guayaquil
Progreso
Pto. Bolívar
Cuenca
Azogues
Cañar
Cañar
Macas
Huasaga
Pastaza
Bobonaza

Sta. Rosa
Machala
Pasaje
Girón
Sigsig
Gral. L. Plaza Gutierrez
Andoas

Pto. Pizarro
Arenillas
Zarumilla
Co. Minas
Gualaquiza
Zamora
Santiago

Tumbes
Zorritos
Piñas
Puyango
Zaruma
Saraguro
Jiménez Banda

4°
Cañaveral
Catacocha
Celica
Loja
Zamora
Co. Tunanta
Cod. del Condor
PERÚ

Macará
Cariamanga
Embl. Poechos
Ayabaca
Amaluza

Sullana
Zumba

Legend:
——	Major sealed highways
——	Other roads
– –	Tracks
——	Railway
▲	Active volcanoes
+	Scheduled air service

Based on the 'Contemporary
Reference Map of South America
1:5 000 000' (Sheet 1) and adapted
for this publication.

m
4000
3000
2000
1000
500
200
0

COLOMBIA

Once a 'país amazónico', Ecuador lost much of its
'oriente' to Perú – especially after the war of
1941 – and is now actively seeking return of the
area shaded in red.

QUITO
PUTUMAYO
CAQUETA
NEGRO

BRASIL

NAPO
GUAYAQUIL
CUENCA
TIGRE
PEBAS
ICA
AMAZONAS

PASTAZA
IQUITOS
LETICIA

PIURA
MARAÑON
PERÚ
JURUA

© 1984 Kevin Healey